Larry Kreider presents a compelling vision for a new way of increasing the effectiveness of the church in his latest book, *House Church Networks: A Church for a New Generation*. Actually, he reports on what God is doing. And when God is up to something new in the church, we better listen! Larry explains why there is a need for the change, without being critical or extreme. I highly recommend this book to all those desirous of releasing more leaders and reaching more people.

Floyd McClung, senior pastor, Metro Christian Fellowship, Kansas City, MO

God is going to change the forms and expressions of church within one generation to a great degree. I believe the house church network is a vital ingredient in that change. Larry's book clearly opens our eyes to see how house churches are needed to model a new kind of church for the next generation.

Mike Bickle, director of International House of Prayer of Kansas City

House Church Networks: A Church For a New Generation is a blueprint for the church of North America for the next decade. Larry speaks from the heart of the Father about the issues facing the new wineskin of the church in the home. I highly recommend this book to every church leader. It will redefine your focus and mission and head you into the next decade with the Holy Spirit.

Rev. Michael Steele, DAWN Ministries, Colorado Springs, Colorado

For years I have been seeing this house church movement coming. I see groups of people who do not fit into church the way we are doing it. They are not angry with the church but just know that there is a better way to reach their own friends with the message of Jesus. Then I heard Larry Kreider and read his manuscript. It ignited me. Larry is on to something. These are brothers and sisters who, like the church in the first century, will never build a building. They will use existing buildings—homes, store-fronts, coffeehouses, businesses. This "new breed" is not interested in turning away from our brothers and sisters in what Larry calls mega-churches and community churches. They will work together. Larry's book needs to be read by every Christian leader in the West. We must understand each other and challenge each other to love God with all our hearts and to love each other even as our Messiah challenged us to do.

Don Finto, Belmont Church, Nashville, Tennessee

In this day where the church is more affected by culture than the other way around, Larry Kreider once again calls us to deeply examine the life-style of Christianity, clearly presented in the book of Acts, but now somehow seemingly out of our reach. With the wise heart of a father and the boldness that comes from truth, Larry is releasing to us the Lord's call to real Christianity.

Robert Stearns, Executive Director, Eagles Wings Ministries, New York City, NY

Larry Kreider has done it again! He has an uncanny ability to see what the future of the church will look like and gives biblical principles that will show many the way forward. He lives what he teaches, and writes with humility and a genuine love for all of God's church. This book will be important for church leaders around the globe, especially for those from the emerging generations. Many will thank Larry for having the courage to declare a new thing before it is widely understood. They will find boldness to lead out because Larry does not put "Saul's armor" on them. He makes church practical and do-able for the layperson.

Jim Orred, Youth With A Mission, Hawaii

Larry's book on the emerging house church movement is timely. Someone said during a pastors' conference: "Friends, in 15 years, your own kids will not pastor churches-as-we-know-it, but lead networks of house churches." I believe this statement to be wrong on the time-side—it will happen much, much earlier. It's time to get ready, now, and Larry's book will help you break into quite new and exciting territory.

Wolfgang Simson, author of Houses That Change the World, strategy advisor of DAWN International, Germany

Larry Kreider is a man with a passion, and that passion shapes and drives this useful new book. Starting from his own extensive background in having helped plant many churches of the cell church model, Larry moves the reader on to a new paradigm which the Lord is raising up all over the world. This paradigm is capturing the simplicity of the most rapidly growing churches worldwide, namely, the house churches. The issue is not that one, and only one model is "best," but rather, what is the Holy Spirit doing with the Lord's people and how do we respond to what we see the Holy Spirit doing.

Dr. Tony Dale, church planter, editor House2House magazine, Austin, Texas

Captivated with vision from a Father's heart, Larry models for us how to make a place for a New Testament form of church that is relevant for our times.

Keith E. Yoder, Teaching The Word Ministries, Pennsylvania

As we have entered the new millennium, there is a heart cry for church wineskins that will be flexible enough to hold the new wine that God is pouring out and produce authentic Christianity on the earth. In this book, Larry Kreider powerfully explores the development of these new wineskins and provides great insight into the journey that the church in western culture is on.

Tony Fitzgerald, Church of the Nations, Virginia

God has repeatedly birthed new wineskins throughout church history. While each new skin retains the essence of New Testament Christianity and kingdom qualities, they also differ in their organizational structures. *House Church Networks: A Church For a New Generation* will be encouraging and thought-provoking reading as the current move of God once again brings change to the church.

Barry L. Wissler, Ephrata Community Church, Pennsylvania

Larry writes as a seasoned symphony composer, harmonizing the unfolding church strategies inspired by the Lord for kingdom advancement in this crucial hour. Larry's futuristic insights regarding the emerging house church networks, channeled through the lens of his successful mega-church and cell-church experience, are balanced and invaluable. Every visionary church leader with a heart for promoting unity in diversity will be richly inspired and instructed by *House Church Networks: A Church For a New Generation.*

Wes Clemmer, Liberty Fellowship of Churches and Ministries, Pennsylvania

I have had the privilege of transitioning a program-based church to a cell-based church. As a result, we have seen wonderful fruit and growth in the lives of God's people. Yet, I sense in my heart another change coming. I believe God is speaking to many church leaders to reach the next generation and Larry is giving us, in his new book, a clear, God-given vision for another "new wineskin" to accomplish this task. I highly recommend this book to all the church leaders who long for the coming harvest.

Paul Gustitus, Indianapolis Christian Fellowship, Indiana

House Church Networks

A church for
a new generation

Larry Kreider

House to House Publications
1924 West Main Street · Ephrata, PA 17522

DEDICATION

To our Lord Jesus Christ, the author and finisher of our faith, and to the next generation of Christian leaders whose sole purpose in life is to know Jesus Christ, obey His voice and desire to please Him while modeling church life according to the pattern of the New Testament.

CONTENTS

ACKNOWLEDGMENTS

A special word of thanks goes to Karen Ruiz, my editor, who tirelessly helped me to write this manuscript.

Thank you, Sarah Mohler, for your skilled cover design and layout expertise.

Another grateful thanks is extended to proofreaders Greg Baird, Katrina Brechbill and Carolyn Sprague.

I also wish to express my appreciation to the DOVE Christian Fellowship International family worldwide for their openness to the Holy Spirit as He continues to lead us and the rest of the body of Christ into our Lord's purposes during these strategic days.

FOREWORD

Are you ready for the news of a new wineskin? If you are, you have the right mindset to absorb the fascinating information packed into the book that you now hold in your hands.

Change today is a way of life. It wasn't always like that however. Back when Jesus talked to the disciples of John the Baptist about new wineskins, changes of any significance were few and far between. Each new first century generation was virtually a carbon copy of the past generation. But no longer. Changes in our society today are not only more frequent but they are also more radical than they have ever been before. Those of us who want to hear what the Spirit is saying to the churches need to keep our ears tuned constantly to what is going on.

Larry Kreider is one who has a long track record of keeping his ears tuned to the new moves of God. Because of this, I, for one, take very seriously what he tells us in this book about the emerging new networks of house churches. House churches aren't exactly new because for the first couple hundred years of the Christian movement, all churches were house churches. However, they have not been the most common form of churches in our generation (with the exception of China), so it is very important for us to understand what they look like and how they operate. They are in the process of becoming a permanent and very visible feature on the landscape of faith these days.

New wineskins are emerging so rapidly that we are getting used to living with not just one new wineskin at a time, but with a variety of new wineskins. That is why Larry makes the important point that, besides house church networks, we also have community churches and mega-churches. He says that all three are needed today. It reminds me of the title of one of Gary McIntosh's church growth books, *One Size Doesn't Fit All*. Just as people prefer different kinds of cars and different kinds of toothpaste and different kinds of homes, the same people will be won to Christ in different kinds of churches. For growing numbers of the new generation, house churches, not the traditional church, will most likely draw them to God.

I would like to suggest that the kinds of churches you will read about in this book may well turn out to be the most effective bases for evangelism in the years to come. I say this because, of all the different kinds of churches, house churches will be most closely attached to the marketplace. When these churches meet, their meeting place does not necessarily have to be a home, although that may be the most common venue. But they can just as well meet in boardrooms, in warehouses, in locker rooms, in restaurants or on construction sites. There are few boundaries to their creativity. Many agree that the most effective evangelists of the future will be marketplace ministers. While some of these will be based in traditional churches, many of them will find that house churches fit much better.

If this is new to you, Larry Kreider will quickly bring you up to speed in *House Church Networks: A Church for a New Generation*. If you already know something about house churches, be ready for new insights, new methods and new suggestions for creative networking. This inspirational and enlightening book has come at just the right time, and I enthusiastically recommend that you read and absorb it. You won't regret the experience!

C. Peter Wagner, Chancellor Wagner Leadership Institute

1

There's a New Church Emerging!

It is happening again. A new species of church is emerging throughout North America. In major cities as well as rural areas, a unique kind of church life is peeking through like the fresh growth of new crops pressing through the surface of the soil.

Hungry for community and relationship, people are learning the values of the kingdom by first-hand participation. They meet in small groups in homes, offices, boardrooms or restaurants. For them church has become a way of life where discipleship and growth occurs naturally as everyone develops their gifts and "learns by doing," under the mentorship of spiritual fathers and mothers. I like to call this fledgling grassroots phenomenon "house church networks."

Within the next ten to fifteen years, I believe these new *house church networks* will dot the landscape of North America just as they already do in other nations of the world. Places like China, central Asia, Latin America, India and Cambodia have experienced tremendous growth through house churches that disciple and empower each member to "be the church."

They are called *house churches* because each one functions as a little church. They are *networks* because they work together to foster accountability and encouragement. Although the terminology *house church networks* may sound like a contemporary concept, they are not really new; in fact, house churches are as old as the book of Acts.

The New Testament *church* was defined as the *people*. Believers did not *go* to church or *join* the church; they *were* the church. All members functioned as priests because everyone served as ministers. Each person got on-the-job-training and learned how to make disciples. These followers of Christ practiced their faith in spiritual families, met in homes and radically changed their world. They grew in number as they obeyed God's Word and shared resources and spiritual blessings. They multiplied into more and more groups of believers meeting in homes, all networking together. These were the original house church networks!

Recently, new house church networks have sprung up throughout North America—from Denver, Colorado to Austin, Texas; from Richmond, Virginia to Portland, Oregon; from Ontario to British Columbia and dozens of places in between. House church networks are emerging rapidly and in growing numbers!

The constant need for new wineskins

Although there are already thousands upon thousands of healthy, vibrant churches throughout North America and the world, new wineskins are continually needed to accommodate the believers who do not fit into the current church structures. House church networks, many believe, will help to restore the simplicity of the New Testament church to the contemporary church.

I had the privilege of serving as a senior pastor of a church for fifteen years. In 1980, our new rural church plant in south central Pennsylvania grew from 25 people to over 1,000 within seven years. By 1990, we had grown to over 2,300. It was truly a miracle of grace. Back then, we thought we had a radical outlook on doing church because we incorporated cell groups as our foundational structure. However, after several years, it became apparent that there was a sense of unrest in our growing church.

I especially noticed this with some of the young people. They craved a new type of wineskin that would provide a more contemporary venue in which to get involved. They were saying the same kind of things we had said ten years earlier: "We are looking for something new. We need something that truly meets our needs." Our ten-year-old wineskin had begun to age—it was past its prime for many of the younger generation.

It didn't take long to conclude that we must find ways to plant new churches (new wineskins) and begin the process of handing over the reins to the next generation. If we didn't, we would lose what we already had. How then could we reach out to our world and reap a harvest? As Dr. Peter Wagner has said so often, "The single most effective way to evangelize is to plant new churches." [1]

DAWN (Discipling A Whole Nation) Ministries, a saturation church planting organization, agrees. This kind of church planting infiltration, that envisions a Christ-centered congregation of believers in every neighborhood in every nation, will deeply affect our society. They suggest that one church is needed for every 500-1,000 people, and our current and prevailing church models will not be able to do it without the influence of these house churches. [2]

New house churches networking effectively together in our communities will give the opportunity for thousands of new churches to be planted rapidly all across the nations of the world. Many more new churches are needed to care for the harvest of souls coming into God's kingdom. Now is the time to prepare.

Both young and old want involvement in church life but fail to find their niche

Just like the generations before them, many of today's young people of Generation X, (18-35 year olds), look at the existing wineskins and have no enthusiasm for them. In my discussions with men and women of this age group over the past five years, throughout North America and in various nations, this is what I hear said repeatedly, "I love Jesus. I love my pastor. I am not rebellious, but I just do not feel like I can enthusiastically give myself to my church." Young people are looking for a church experience that will give them a reason to get involved and motivate them to enthusiastically participate.

It is not just Generation X that backs away from full participation in church life because they do not feel needed in the larger crowd. Older people, too, are looking for a new model of church where they can be fully involved. I can still vividly remember a man in his 50's confiding in me, with tears running down his cheeks, after I taught at his megachurch: "I know the Lord called me years ago to be a pastor, but I just do not know how it can ever happen here in my church."

This man, who gave relationships high priority, was a loving person with a pastor's heart. He was longing to fulfill God's call on his life.

Think what could happen if he had a house church venue. As a spiritual father in a house church, he could fulfill his heart's cry. In a house church, he could look after his spiritual extended family and find his niche.

Therefore, it is not just the younger generation that house churches appeal to. However, overall, I believe it will be the younger generation that will take the lead in starting new house churches and house church networks in our communities. Why? Because they will thrive in a new wineskin that fits their generation's need for authentic relationships. Young adults are very open to small groups that are based on friendships and socializing. They love to spend time in homes and in discussion. This young generation especially craves real-life connections because it is a generation raised in the non-physical oriented communication structures of cyberspace:

> ...our culture once based exclusively on physical contact is being transformed to one where goods and services are accessible without face-to-face contact with other people. Technology enables this transformation... [3]

Although the Internet creates an online community with email, instant messaging, newsgroups and the ability to run a home business on the Web, physical human contact is a vital missing element. Technology, however helpful, like PC's, palm pilots, cell phones and a multitude of other gadgets at this generation's fingertips, do not inspire deep relational connections. This generation is looking for dependable, meaningful relationships.

God wants to connect the generations

In addition to a connection with their peers, young people are looking for significant interaction with the older generations. They desire spiritual fathers and mothers who will come alongside them, encourage, and support their dreams and efforts.

God longs to connect the generations in healthy relationships so they can work together in unity and oneness to advance His kingdom. In the book, *The Cry for Spiritual Fathers & Mothers*, I explain why God desires this connection:

God's intention is to raise spiritual parents who are willing to nurture spiritual children and help them grow up in their Christian lives. This is a fulfillment of the Lord's promise in the last days to "turn the hearts of the fathers to the children, and the hearts of the children to their fathers..." (Malachi 4:6).

The Lord wants to restore harmony among fathers and their children, both naturally and spiritually, so fathers can freely impart their inheritance to the next generation...with the old and the young working together, a mighty and ongoing spiritual legacy will multiply and endure. Imparting spiritual fatherhood fills the void and closes the gap of broken relationships between the old and the young.[4]

The generations must learn to work together. The heart's cry of the older generation must be to release the younger generation to fulfill the Lord's call on their lives.

More than twenty years ago, a man of God named Dan Yutzy, a church leader and professor from Taylor University, turned to a group of Mennonite bishops in Lancaster County, Pennsylvania, and spoke a word about the younger leadership represented: "We must release these young men and let them go!" He knew the new generation needed to be trusted to start new church structures to accommodate the new Christians coming into the kingdom. I was a product of this decision.

Along with a few other zealous young people, we started a new cell-based church in rural south central Pennsylvania that had a different structure to it than the other churches in the community. At first, some of the local church pastors thought we were a cult because this new wineskin looked so different with its emphasis on believers meeting in cell groups in homes during the week. Additionally, at our Sunday morning services, our charismatic style of worship was livelier than some of the more traditional churches in our community. One Baptist pastor later said he thought we "swung from chandeliers." In retrospect, if there had been a chandelier, we probably would have swung from it!

Each generation needs to find its fit

Why did we start this new cell-based church in our community? There was a growing need for it. The young believers that came to

Christ through friendship evangelism were not fitting into the churches in our community. These churches had traditions the new Christians could not relate to. To accommodate these new believers, it became apparent that the new Christians would need a new structure in which to grow.

Jesus said, "And no one pours new wine into old wineskins. If he does, the new wine will burst the skins, the wine will run out and the wineskins will be ruined. No, new wine must be poured into new wineskins" (Luke 5:37-38). The new Christians are like new wine, still in the process of fermentation. When put in old wineskins (existing church structures), they may not be compatible.

Every generation needs to be free to discover and discern which wineskin is best for them. I like the way Leonard Sweet explains it in his book *Aqua Church*:

> My wife is a tea drinker. Her favorite container is a little cup with a handle so tiny I can't even get my finger through it. My favorite container is a Jadite coffee mug (I started collecting Fire King Jadite long before Martha Stewart inflated the market and made it uncollectible). Our eight-year-old Thane's favorite container is a little glass we put juice in. Our three-year-old Soren's favorite container is a Winnie the Pooh sippy cup. Eighteen-month-old Egil's favorite container is a bottle.
>
> Every generation needs a shape that fits its own hands, its own soul. Each generation, every person, needs a different handle from which to receive the living waters of Jesus. Our task is to pour the living water into anything anyone will pick up. By "anything," I mean that literally: anything. If I want to reach my twenty-second century children (they probably will live to see 2100) with the gospel of Jesus, I must be prepared to pour the living water into containers of which I myself would never be caught dead drinking. This is what Paul meant when he talked about our "becoming all things to all men" that we might win some (1 Corinthians 9:22). [5]

Once again, the generation of today needs a unique "shape that fits its hands." They need to be released to find that shape.

Recently, I spoke at a leadership conference at a large church in the United States, and a woman said to me, "Every week, my home is filled with a twenty-something crowd of young people. They are not the kind of kids that fit in the traditional church. I know they are experiencing church right in my home, but I do not want to be competitive to my church or be misunderstood. However, I see that we are becoming *the church* as a body of believers." Many others face this same dilemma. They are experiencing dynamic church in a home, but need to be released to really *be* the church.

A new wineskin is emerging; let's not resist it. It may change the way church looks today. Let's open our hearts to the new wineskins God is preparing so the new and the old can work together to advance His kingdom.

Find a way "back to the future"

A popular science fiction film called *Back to the Future* tells the story of a young man accidentally sent back in time. In the past, he learns vital information for the future, but must find a way to get "back to the future" intact.

Perhaps we should take a step back in time to learn from the New Testament church to help us solve problems for some of our modern-day church dilemmas. House churches in the western world are really in their infancy stage. We have a lot to learn, but we have an excellent pattern to follow from the New Testament. The Lord will lead us step by step.

The book of Proverbs tells us, "My child, don't lose sight of good planning and insight. Hang on to them. For they will fill you with life and bring you honor and respect" (Proverbs 3:21-22 NLT). For thousands of believers throughout the world, His plan might very well include their involvement in a house church network.

Notes
1   C. Peter Wagner, *Church Planting For a Greater Harvest,* (Regal 1990), p. 11
2   "Proposal for a House Church Network," www.dawn.ch
3   Paul Gray and Magid Igbaria, "The Virtual Society," *OR/MS Today,* December 1996, p. 44
4   Larry Kreider, *The Cry for Spiritual Fathers & Mothers*, (Ephrata, PA: House to House Publications, 2000), pp. 3,4
5   Leonard Sweet, *Aqua Church,* (Loveland, Colorado: Group, 1999), pp. 28-29

A New Form of Church For a New Generation

Before we take a closer look at this growing, worldwide grassroots movement of house church networks, we have to clarify an important point. *House churches* should not be confused with *cell churches* currently found in many communities today.

How "cell churches" function

More than two decades ago, a new wineskin called *cell church* started to flourish to meet a growing need within the contemporary church. Many people realized traditional church methods were not meeting modern believers' needs. The church was building-bound, clergy-centered, and many Christians longed for a place to belong and be effective witnesses to the gospel. Churches soon realized that small groups (cell groups) could help people rediscover that they could "do the work of ministry." Left behind was a spectator mentality of church where the pastor did all the work.

In the ensuing years, many churches utilized small groups that gave everyone a job to do. Everyone's talents and gifts were exercised to benefit others, and people were able to gain on-the-job training for leadership through hands-on experiences.

The cell groups also provided a more natural setting for evangelism since they gave the opportunity to do evangelism as a team. Together the cell group could pray for God to use their group to reach the people of their personal *oikos* (from the Greek word *household* in the Bible. Our *oikos* are those people with whom we relate on a regular basis— our co-workers, our families, those with whom we share a common interest such as sports or music, our dentist, our car mechanic, etc.). In a cell group setting, nonbelievers were more easily drawn in and found a place to be loved and cared for.

With the cell system made famous through David Yonggi Cho's successful church in Korea, multitudes of *cell churches* emerged on the scene and cut through all denominational lines. Some churches started as new cell-based churches, other churches transitioned to cell-based ministry and still others simply developed cell groups within their current church structure. Today most every denomination has some kind of cell group ministry operating within their church structure that aims to be a place where ministry and caring takes place on a more personal level.

However, current cell churches continue to function mainly within the traditional church structure. In other words, although believers meet during the week in homes, in many cases these cell groups still function as complementary ministries to the larger Sunday church meeting. A senior pastor leads this larger gathering and also oversees all the leadership under him in the cell groups. This structure, of larger meetings and smaller cell meetings, requires many cell leaders, assistants and zone pastors, all of whom are accountable to the senior pastor and his leadership team. Additionally, a cell-based church or church with cells also requires a headquarters or a church building to accommodate the various church functions.

How "house churches" function

House churches are entirely different. Although they meet in homes like cell groups, that's where much of the similarity ends. According to my friend Wolfgang Simson in his challenging and cutting-edge book, *Houses that Change the World*, house churches are not mere appendages of the larger church, but real, *bona fide* churches:

> [Both] concepts look similar, but are really miles apart, because they build on different values, and a different understanding of church. Where the home group is a small part of the big and "real" church, a "mini-version" of the church, the

house church in itself is the church in its fullest and most holistic sense.[1]

Unlike the cell-based church or church with cells, each house church is meant to be a complete little church. Each church is led not by a cell leader and a team of assistant leaders, but by a spiritual father or mother who functions as the elder along with a small eldership team for the little church. He or she does not simply lead a meeting in a house, but rather provides an environment for people to grow spiritually in the context of everyday life. There is no need for a church building in which to meet because each house church is a fully functioning church in itself, meeting in a home.

This is not to say that a house church consists of only one group meeting in a house. A house church should encourage smaller "cells" within the group to meet for prayer, encouragement and accountability outside of the actual house church meeting. One "cell" of people could regularly meet for breakfast before work and another "cell" could meet together to disciple a few new Christians in the house church.

House churches are simple to start, provide a natural setting for ministry, and are easily replicated. Could these new churches meeting in homes, places of business, coffee shops—anywhere people meet, be the new look of the modern church?

House churches are a relevant way to engage our communities with the claims of Jesus, according to a successful house church network in Canada:

House churches are simple, easily reproducible, create platforms for gift identification and development, and are effective in showing forth the transforming power of Christ in our neighborhoods and our communities. The postmodern anti-institutional mind, which will not enter traditional church, will come to my home. The Muslim or Hindu neighbor may not go to church, but they will enjoy Canadian hospitality. In the context of everyday life, the message and meaning of the gospel can be communicated in effective ways.[2]

Like the New Testament church, the house church network focuses on relationships, reaching the lost and raising spiritual fathers and mothers in-house who serve and care for their family. It emerges as a wonderfully fluid and flexible church. Small house churches are expanding rapidly because they meet a desperate need in church life today.

"Search for the right church ends at home"

The above line was the title of a *New York Times* article by Laurie Goodstein who interviewed David Ketchum, from Massachusetts, who admits that for the last 12 years, he "dragged his wife and four children from church to church in a fruitless search for the ideal fellowship. Every time the new Yellow Pages came," said Mr. Ketchum, an elementary school teacher, "I would open it up to *churches* to see if there were any new ones I hadn't been to yet."

His search has found an end, in Wayne and Charlene Wilder's house church, almost on his doorstep. They have no pews, no choir and no pastor, only armchairs and other people seeking deeper Christian fellowship than they found in institutionalized churches. Professor Nancy T. Ammerman, sociologist of religion at Hartford Seminary, Connecticut, comments, "this development shows people looking for faith's essence. They are no longer willing to finance huge buildings, a large staff, insurance policies, advertising campaigns and the leaking church roof, because it all seems simply irrelevant." According to the *New York Times* report, an increasing number of Christians in the United States think like the Ketchums, and are setting to work themselves. The result is "do-it-yourself" churches in people's homes. Over 1,600 such house churches can be found on Web pages in the United States alone.[3]

House churches network and reproduce rapidly

Some call the new wineskin emerging a new Reformation because it will radically change the look of *church* as we know it in our communities. This new kind of church meets in homes, where believers gather at least once each week to relate and minister to each other informally. These are actual churches, not just Bible studies or cell groups. They have elders, they collect tithes and offerings, and the leadership is responsible before the Lord for the souls of the people in the house church (Hebrews 13:17).

Each "house church," although a little church in itself, is committed to network with other house churches in their city or region. This keeps them from pride, exclusiveness and heresy. Several new house church leaders I know (many in their 20's and 30's), tell me that their new house churches are planning to meet together once every month or so for corporate worship and teaching because they recognize the need to be connected. This desire to network comes from a similar desire to receive oversight from spiritual fathers and mothers so they stay accountable.

Additionally, these young leaders are intent on the rapid reproduction of these house churches. When they outgrow the house or place where they are meeting, instead of constructing a church building, they plant a new house church. Sounds a bit like the book of Acts, doesn't it?

A new form of church for a new generation

House church networks especially appeal to the young people of *Generation X,* because they offer the kind of casual and informal church experience to which they can relate. We need these new kinds of churches because they fit the heart, call and passion of the younger generations. Earlier this year, *Religion Today* published an article entitled, "Look Out, Here Comes the Gen-X Church." Here is what they had to say:

> ...Generation X Christians are radically changing the church....The generation of 18 to 35-year-olds, less concerned about structure and hierarchy, are disconnected from traditional churches and starting small, informal fellowships....The churches meet in homes, coffee shops, warehouses, fast-food restaurants, industrial complexes, parks, and other unconventional places. Relationships are the key...Generations Xers are loyal to each other over and above anything else. Sometimes this is a fault, when feelings receive higher ratings than the message. But this has not yet given rise to any major concerns of youth culture heresy. What usually happens is that this commitment to each other translates into loving concern, which is the key redemptive characteristic of the culture.[4]

We must change the way we "do church"

In his book, *Boiling Point,* George Barna, a specialist in research on the Christian church and its effectiveness in our modern civilization, takes an in-depth look at the changing beliefs and attitudes of society today and how Christians must anticipate the world's spiritual needs. One of the innovations he suggests for "doing church" is to offer the house church as a structure for restoring community and authenticity to the church:

> Popular in other countries, especially Southeast Asia, thousands of independent faith groups will meet for a complete church experience and expression within living rooms and garages...this option will appeal to individuals who are especially interested in restoring authenticity, community and simplicity to the church.[5]

Barna's extensive studies of the pervading culture cause him to see clearly that the gaping deficiencies of today's church fail to fulfill the needs of today's generation. There are many others who also believe the church of the future will undergo a face change. Many believe the young people of today will be the first ones to embrace this change. "Just wait for it," says Karsten Wolf, a youth church pastor from Germany. "Today's Generation X is tomorrow's mainstream society. What we are doing to change the way we experience church will greatly impact the way we 'do church' in the future," he maintains. He believes the youth culture churches of today will define the church of the future. Consider that:

1. Generation X is the largest single generation in the history of mankind, numbering in the region of a couple billion.

2. With the global media beaming the same message to the same generation worldwide, young people (aged 18-35) are more the same in their thinking today than ever before.

3. As this generation ages and—within the next decade— becomes the prevailing society, they will bring their changes with them. Whatever Generation X has done to the church will be lasting and normative.

"The young people of today, in 10 years or less, will be the society of the nations. That's why, if we shape new models of church today, we are shaping the church of the future. Youth culture churches may well revolutionize what church becomes in the future. We could be looking at an absolutely new form of church. I think we will need this new form of church to reach the nations," says Wolf. [6]

Not only for the younger generation!

Let me emphasize that although the house church network appeals especially to the young, there are thousands of other "young at heart" people with the same vision burning in their hearts. Recently, I was with a couple in their early 70's from Hamilton, New Zealand, who are planting a new church in their home. They came to faith in Christ at the age of fifty. After having served faithfully in their community church for the past twenty years, they are now ready to launch out to plant a new church in their home with a vision from the Lord to see it multiply into a network of New Testament-like house churches in their community.

Believers are longing to find their place

I meet many believers, especially in North America, who have spent the past 20-30 years with a sense of unrest in their spirits. They love the Lord, but are discouraged. A couple of decades ago, they experienced a new wave of the Spirit sweeping across North America. They envisioned a radical New Testament church experience emerging from this spiritual renewal, but cumbersome church structure and traditional church meetings and procedures frustrated the dream. Now they find themselves in a "holding pattern." They dream of experiencing life-changing discipleship that transforms society around them, but they are not experiencing anything close to it now.

Deep in their spirits, they believe the Lord is about to make some radical changes in His church. They have been looking for something new, yet unsure of what they are looking for. They are passionately in love with Jesus, but feel unable to find their niche in the body of Christ.

Don't isolate! Find that connection

Some have become disillusioned, others have been hurt or are even bitter toward the church, feeling they are right and the rest of the church is wrong. They meet in their homes with like-minded believers, cut off from the rest of the body of Christ. There are entire books written advocating this type of unwholesome behavior.

We must "beware of authors who live in anger toward the established church," says Ralph Moore who is responsible for planting dozens of Hope Chapel churches throughout Hawaii and the west coast of the United States. "The anger of man still can't work the righteousness of God." [7] I totally agree.

House churches, and churches of any kind, should never be exclusive entities cut off from the rest of the body of Christ. The litmus test used to discern if a house church is healthy is simple. The healthy house church will focus on loving the Lord, loving each other, reaching the lost and loving the rest of the body of Christ anywhere and everywhere.

Jesus "came to seek and to save what was lost" (Luke 19:10), and He prayed that we would be one as the Father and the Son are one (John 17:21). Healthy believers will want to relate closely to the rest of the body of Christ because they want to be "one with the Father and each other."

God offers a richness through different Christian faith expressions. Each kind of church contributes its strengths to the others. We need each other. God uses different types of churches to accomplish His purposes. Each part of the church, regardless of denominational labels or structure, is a vital part of the body of Christ. God works through all of His people, giving us a sense of the broader community of Christ's body.

In the next chapters, we will look more closely at how God is working through His people in all of the current models of church life.

Notes
[1] Wolfgang Simson, *Houses that Change the World,* (Cumbria, UK: OM Publishing, 1998), p. 94
[2] Bob Granholm, "Proposal for a House Church Network in the Lower Mainland (British Columbia, Canada)," October 1999, www.dawn.ch
[3] Laurie Goodstein, *New York Times*, "Search for the Right Church Ends at Home," April 2001
[4] *Religion Today*, "Look Out, Here Comes the Gen-X Church," January 2001
[5] George Barna & Mark Hatch, *Boiling Point,* (Ventura, CA: Regal, 2001), p. 250
[6] www.dawnministries.org/europe
[7] *House2House Magazine*, March 2001, p. 20

Today's Community Churches and Mega-Churches

The Lord is using diversified types of structures to build His church today. From the traditional church to the emerging house church networks, God's Spirit is being poured out on His people. Our God is a God of infinite creativity and variety; you see it in His creation, from the long-necked graceful giraffe to the multicolored butterfly. You see His variety in the shades of skin color of His people and the multitude of talents and gifts He gives. God had no interest in producing clones when He created our world.

It's my conviction that He continues to bless variety and creativity in His church today by the many different structures and methods He uses to accomplish His purposes. Although I sincerely believe the new house church networks are tailor-made for today's generation and will be a force in returning to the New Testament model of church life, I also believe God is using today's conventional church structures—what I call the community churches and mega-churches—to play their part in God's future plan. God will build His kingdom regardless of our models, structure or plans.

Both those churches that operate within a more traditional setting and those that operate outside of traditional structures are needed. It is a big job to equip the saints for ministry and bring the gospel to a lost and dying world. We need everyone to work together, allowing the new and the old to coexist and complement each other.

In this chapter and the next, we will look at three necessary types of healthy churches found in the nations today: the community churches, the mega-churches and the house church networks. Their combined strengths will contribute to bringing about God's kingdom here on earth as it is in heaven!

Three kinds of churches today: community churches, mega-churches, and house church networks

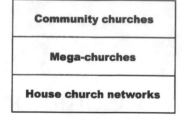

The community church

In nearly every community around the world, you can find what I like to call "community churches." Most of these churches meet in a church facility each Sunday morning, in addition to holding various meetings at the church building throughout the week. There are many styles and flavors of community churches. There is the Methodist flavor, the Baptist flavor, the Congregational flavor, the Episcopal flavor, the Presbyterian flavor, the Vineyard flavor, the Assembly of God flavor, the non-denominational flavor, the independent flavor; the list goes on and on. Some are Calvinistic; some are Arminian. Some are Charismatic in their worship expression, while some are traditional. Some churches are dispensational in their theology, while others focus on the here and now. Some churches are cell-based, and others are not. Some are "seeker-sensitive"—geared for those new to Christianity, while others appeal to the mature Christian with extended times of worship and the exercising of spiritual gifts. Nearly every Sunday somewhere in the world, I have the privilege of speaking at one of these community churches with their different flavors. I love the many unique expressions of the body of Christ. It would be boring if each expression looked exactly the same!

My family and I live in rural Lancaster County, Pennsylvania. In this county alone, there are more than 600 community churches of every kind imaginable. The great majority of those churches have between 50 and 200 members. Some have 400 to 500 or even 800 to 900 people. When they reach approximately 1,000 attendees, they fall into another classification—the mega-church—which will be examined later.

Although community churches range in size, they all have a clear target area they are reaching—the local populace. In many cases, those that attend and those they reach live in the general geographical area.

Community churches are like community stores

The community church reminds me of the local community store. Where do you buy your groceries? You probably shop at a local grocery store in your community. It might be an independent store, or it could be part of a large chain of stores, but it is the store closest in proximity to where you live. You may personally know the clerks, and you know where specific items are shelved.

Some neighborhood stores, like community churches, are larger than others, but they still feel like a community store. This store serves your local area. Very few people in your neighborhood would drive a long distance to get their groceries. Some even walk to a corner grocery store.

The community church like a community store

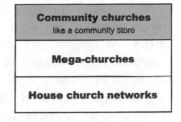

Likewise, very few people will drive long distances to worship with other believers who gather each week at their community church facility. Proximity and ease of access are a big part of the very nature of the community church.

More choices

Thirty years ago, nearly every church in America was a community church (generally a church of 50-1,000 in attendance). There were very few exceptions. Then something happened. American Christians and American pastors started to hear reports about churches in places like Seoul, Korea, that were massive. We heard that there were over 100,000 people in Yoido Full Gospel Church in Seoul.

Dr. Yonggi Cho, pastor of the world's largest church in Seoul, came to America to explain how pastors in America can also have large churches by "praying and obeying." He taught these church leaders to obey the voice of the Holy Spirit and train small group (cell) leaders and release the ministry of the church to these trained leaders. Through the help of small groups, rapid multiplication and growth occurred.

The mega-church

This new mentality led to a wave of mega-churches mushrooming across America. Many implemented cell groups to help them grow. Victory Christian Center of Tulsa, Oklahoma, whose founding pastor is

Billy Joe Daugherty, is a mega-church that has had cell groups for 20 years. Their weekly Sunday worship attendance is 7,700 and they are now one of the few churches in the world who will break through the 1,000 cell group mark, according to Karen Hurston in her book *Breakthrough Cell Groups.*[1]

Not only did mega-churches like this spring up in major metropolitan areas, they appeared on the rural scene. Today, at least in the United States, it is not unusual for people to drive for an hour or an hour and a half to attend worship services at a mega-church. Mega-churches have much to offer. There are ministries for every member of the family, twelve step programs for those with addictions, Bible schools, concerts, youth ministries, singles' ministries; you name it, almost anything is available. The mega-church phenomenon has changed the face of the church in America.

Popular Bible teacher and bishop, T. D. Jakes, started his mega-church upon relocating his family and 50 other families from West Virginia, to Dallas, Texas, to establish a new church called "The Potter's House." Within eighteen months, it grew to more than 14,000 worshipers! It is one of the nation's fastest-growing mega-churches. *Christianity Today Magazine* notes "other mega-churches such as Saddleback Valley Community Church in Mission Viejo, California, and Willow Creek in South Barrington, Illinois, took several years to become so large." [2]

It is a fact that mega-churches are growing rapidly. According to the National Association of Evangelicals, there are about 189 churches with more than 3,000 average weekly attendance nationwide. In our nation, every two weeks a new church with 2,000 or more members opens.[3]

Our rural area of Lancaster County, Pennsylvania, presently has five mega-churches, each having over 1,000 people in attendance every week with two of these churches having about 3,000 attendees.

Mega-churches are like Wal-Mart superstores!

I like to call the mega-church the "Wal-Mart superstore church." Wal-Mart has taken our nation by storm. Twenty-five years ago, I had never even heard of Wal-Mart since Wal-Mart was mainly a department store chain in the southern part of our nation. Then it invaded northeastern USA where I live. Now Wal-Mart is everywhere! People will drive for an hour or more to shop at a Wal-Mart because they love the low prices, the huge inventory of consumer products and they can get all they need in one place all at the same time.

Mega-churches, like the Wal-Mart superstores, are large and they offer an abundance of services to the churchgoer. However, unlike the community church where you may know nearly everyone, at a mega-church you probably know only a few people. Yet, church members thoroughly enjoy a mega-church since everything is easily accessible in one location.

The mega-church like a Wal-Mart superstore

In 1980, I started pastoring a church that focused on meeting in cell groups in homes during the week and also in Sunday morning services. Using the cell group structure, we continued to multiply our numbers until we were in the mega-church category. Many of us drove an hour or more to attend weekly services on Sunday. There was a Bible school, a dynamic youth ministry, a singles' ministry, and a ministry for those who had gone through a divorce; dozens of short-term mission teams were sent out, plus many other specialized ministries were taking place. Dr. Cho, the pastor of the world's largest church, came to speak at our church for a leadership conference. Our mega-church had the feel of a spiritual Wal-Mart.

Everyone is different, having varying needs, so it's not unusual that some people love Wal-Mart while others seldom if ever shop there. The same is true when people decide which church to attend. Some love the mega-church while others feel lost in the crowd and prefer the smaller community church.

DOVE Christian Fellowship's journey from community church to mega-church

People are the church. Churches of all kinds have a way of springing up and flourishing when people allow the Lord to use them for His purposes. Allow me to share with you the roots of our church as it evolved from a community church to a mega-church.

As I mentioned earlier, I and a few other young people started a cell-based church in our community due to an increasing need for a new wineskin to accommodate the new wine. It all started during the summer of 1971, when my future wife, LaVerne, and I helped to start a youth ministry with a small band of young people who began to reach out to the unchurched youth of our community in northern Lancaster County, Pennsylvania. We played sports and conducted various activities throughout the week for spiritually needy youngsters and teenagers. This kind of friendship evangelism produced results, and during the next few years, dozens of young people came to faith in Christ with a desire to find their place in a local church.

Every Sunday night we took vanloads of these new believers to various churches in our community, because we wanted to help them plug into a local church. After the church services, the entire group usually returned to our home for a time of praise, prayer, spiritual counseling and just plain fun. Our desire was to teach them from the scriptures what practical Christian living was all about.

Those of us who served in this youth ministry were from various local churches, so we sincerely wanted to help the new believers find their place in our local congregations. We quickly discovered that the Christians in the local churches were friendly and helpful, but these new believers were not getting connected. The young believers simply were not being assimilated into the life of the established churches in our communities.

The need for flexible wineskins

The answer to the dilemma came when a church leader shared from Matthew 9:16-17 concerning new wine and wineskins. The "new wineskin" is a new model of church structure, tailored to serve and equip new believers in Jesus Christ.

A wineskin is like a balloon. It needs to be flexible and pliable. Putting new Christians (new wine) into old structures can cause the structures to break and the new Christians may be lost. New Christians should be placed in new structures which are flexible and able to encourage their spiritual growth.

It was clear there was a need for a New Testament church flexible enough to relate to believers from all kinds of backgrounds and assist them in their spiritual growth. So, in October 1980, a group of approximately twenty-five believers met for the first time for a Sunday morning celebration in a living room. "DOVE Christian Fellowship" had officially begun. There was an aura of excitement among us as we also met in three separate home groups during the week. The focus was not on Sunday morning meetings. The focus was on the church meeting from house to house throughout the communities each week.

During the next ten years, the church grew to over 2,300 believers scattered throughout communities in a seven-county area of Pennsylvania. We had now reached the mega-church classification. These believers met in more than 125 cell groups during the week and on Sunday mornings met in clusters of cells (congregations) in five different locations. The whole church came together several times each year on a Sunday morning in a large gymnasium or at a local park amphitheater for a corporate service.

Whenever a congregation's Sunday morning celebration outgrew its rented facility, they either moved to a larger facility or began two or three new celebrations meeting in the same building. Our goal was to multiply the cells and celebrations by beginning new celebrations and new cell groups in other areas as God gave the increase. We also found that by renting buildings at an economical rate, we had more money available to use for world mission. During these years, churches were planted in Scotland, Brazil, Kenya and New Zealand. These overseas churches were built on Jesus Christ and on these same house-to-house principles.

We decided to give our church away

As DOVE Christian Fellowship International (DCFI) grew, it became clear to us that in order for us to accomplish the vision God had given us, we would have to make major adjustments. If we wanted to build the church with a focus of cell groups in the nations of the world, we would have to give the church away. When a father gives his daughter to her husband-to-be on their wedding day, he realizes he has invested many years in training his daughter for this very moment——to give her away.

Therefore, that is exactly what we did with our church. Giving our church away better suited our vision of a cell-based church planting movement intent on training a new generation of church planters and leaders. Our church in south central Pennsylvania became eight individual churches, each with its own eldership team. We formed an Apostolic Council to give oversight to all the churches of DCFI. Then we gave each of the eight celebrations the freedom to become autonomous—they had the option of joining with the DCFI family of churches or connecting to another part of the body of Christ. Each of these eight churches affirmed their desire to join DCFI. Churches that we had helped to plant in Kenya, Uganda, and New Zealand also confirmed their desire to be a part of this new international family of churches.

This time of change was not easy for us. I enjoyed being the senior pastor of a mega-church along with the security it brought. Those of us on the leadership team and staff of DCFI had to walk in a new level of faith for finances. The finances we had received each week from the tithes of one mega-church were now given to each autonomous cell-based church. Of course, obedience always pays off. In the years since the transition, the Lord has always faithfully provided!

DCFI's family of cell-based churches collaborating together grows steadily. We are currently a network of 85 churches on five continents. Together the network is mobilizing and empowering God's people at the grassroots level to fulfill His purposes. DCFI churches are found in the USA, Kenya, Uganda, New Zealand, Scotland, Canada, Barbados, Croatia and Bulgaria. For a complete history of DCFI, see page 108.

New horizons ahead!

When I think of the beginnings of our new church plant in 1980, I realize it actually started as a house church. It had all the components of a little church by itself with leadership raised up in-house. When we made the move to a larger building after outgrowing the living room we were using, the dynamics changed considerably. We needed to develop the "temple ministry" of church life as we met for a larger celebration on a Sunday morning in addition to our small cell groups. The evolution of this change has resulted in a more traditional community church much like the other churches in our area, despite our unique cell-based structure.

Although my experience has been in the life of Christ expressed through the community church and the mega-church, this experience points to far more possibilities for the church to go about its task of discipling the nations. That is why I am excited about the feasibility of house churches. We need to "keep all options open" so the Lord can use all of His servants to function together as one body to change the world.

It's time to "pray and obey" again

Time marches on. What was new and unique several years ago becomes an old wineskin in today's world.

I believe it is time again to pray and obey. Generation X and many others who share their passion and convictions are dreaming of another type of church in America—the house church network. I am so grateful to those who have gone before me. They prepared the way for me—as a young man—to start a unique wineskin that was different from the *status quo*.

A new day has arrived, again. The Lord has been instructing me and many of my generation to prepare the way for the next generation of church planters and church leaders who will model a new type of church for the next generation.

In today's church world, you can find the community store churches and the Wal-Mart superstore churches everywhere. The Lord has and will continue to use both. However, He will also use the new house church networks with their different approaches and structures to build His kingdom. Let's open our hearts to this revolutionary force that is growing quietly in humble house churches across the nation and around the world.

Notes
[1] Karen Hurston, *Breakthrough Cell Groups*, (Houston, TX: Touch Publications, 2001)
[2] Jim Jones, *Christianity Today*, "Swift Growth Shapes Potter's House," January 12, 1998, Vol. 42, No. 1, p. 56
[3] *Ministries Today*, "Ministry Matters," compiled by Eric Tiansay, July/August 2001

New on the Horizon: The House Church Network

Last year, I agreed to home school our sixteen year old son Josh. He had spent eight years in a Christian school and one year in a public school, but he was ready for a change. Initially, when he asked me to consider home schooling him, I thought it would be impossible with my intense travel schedule. However, as my wife LaVerne and I prayerfully considered the possibility, we felt I should go ahead. It has turned out to be a great experience!

Had I told you thirty years ago I was going to home school our son, you would have looked at me strangely. In fact, you may have thought I was getting involved in some type of new cult. If you recall, thirty years ago, home schooling was almost unheard of in America. Nevertheless, early home schooling advocates made their mark on education in America and today home schooling is commonplace and well accepted as an alternative to traditional classroom training. Home schooling is growing at the rate of 15% annually throughout America.[1] Over the past decade, the ranks of families home schooling has grown dramatically, according to *Time Magazine*: "More kids learn at home than attend all the public schools in Alaska, Delaware, Hawaii, Montana, New Hampshire, North Dakota, Rhode Island, South Dakota, Vermont and Wyoming combined." [2]

Don't get me wrong. I am not promoting home schooling as the pinnacle of educational experience, but it certainly is a wonderful choice. Parents today have the choice of home schooling their children, along with the traditional choices of public or private schooling. All three types of educational training coexist in nearly every community in America.

I believe within the next several years, house church networks will mushroom all across America. Like our educational choices, they will coexist and network with other more traditional community churches and mega-churches of our communities meeting in church buildings every Sunday. Our God will use and bless all three—the community churches, the mega-churches, and the house church networks.

House church networks

I previously compared the *community church* to a community store and the *mega-church* to a Wal-Mart superstore. Now let's look at a *house church network*. In describing a house church network, the analogy would be equivalent to the stores in a shopping mall. If the average store found in a shopping mall was taken out of the mall and let to stand on its own, it would die within a year. The normal store in a shopping mall needs the others to survive. Each specialized store flourishes together within the cluster of the others. Yet each store is fully a "store" in its own right, despite being in a mall.

House church networks like a shopping mall with many stores

The house churches function like these shopping mall stores. They are individual and specialized, yet they flourish only when they network together with other house churches. We will explain later how they network, but for now let's look at how each one functions as a real church.

House churches have a unique mentality

The entire concept of house churches requires a different way of thinking than we have been used to. Believers in house churches do not focus on growing larger like the community church or the mega-church. They focus on growth by starting new house churches by multiplication. One way of thinking is not right and the other wrong; they are just different. Remember the Christian school, the public school and the home school. Which is right? They are all right, depending on which place you believe the Lord wants you to be.

Since all are valid, the question remains: Which type of church has the Lord called you to be involved in? Most believers do not even know there are three options, just like home schooling was not a common option thirty years ago. Times, however, have changed.

I agree with Wolfgang Simson who firmly believes that when we "bring the church to people," the church will see greater results:

> The church is changing back from being a Come-structure to being again a Go-structure. As one result, the church needs to stop trying to bring people "into the church," and start bringing the church to people. The mission of the church will never be accomplished just by adding to the existing structure; it will take nothing less than a mushrooming of the church through spontaneous multiplication of itself into areas of the population of the world, where Christ is not yet known.[3]

House churches are small; therefore they can meet anywhere—in a house, in a college dorm room, in a coffee shop, in a corporate board-room. They meet in these locations and do not think of growing larger requiring the construction of a building to accommodate the larger group. Instead, they say, "How can we multiply leaders and start more house churches?" "How can we walk together as house church leaders?"

DAWN Ministries further clarifies this very point:

> The house church is a structure that reflects the core nature of the church—that is, an extension of the spirit of the Father in heaven here on earth. It is a spiritual, enlarged, organic family...it is inherently participatory and not consumer-provider driven.
>
> Its responsibility structure is also very simple and effective: individual house churches are fathered by elders, who in turn are equipped by itinerant servants like those in the fivefold ministry (Ephesians 4:11-13). They often relate to a regional spiritual father-figure, who, through his humble apostolic passion and vision, often becomes something like a "pillar of the church," an anchor-place for a regional movement that fills its cities and villages with the presence of Christ.
>
> Since New Testament times, there has no longer been such a thing as "a house of God." At the cost of his life, Stephen reminded unequivocally: "God does not live in temples made by

human hands." The church is the people of God. The church, therefore, was and is at home where people are at home: in ordinary houses.[4]

Modern-day house church networks

During the past few years, thousands of new small "house churches" that network together have sprung up throughout the world. I was in China recently where over 80 million believers are part of house church networks. More than 2,000 house churches led by Generation X have sprung up throughout Western Europe. Southern Baptist missionaries have started thousands of them in Latin America, India, and Southeast Asia. House church networks have already emerged in the United States in Denver, Dallas, Austin, Cincinnati, San Francisco, and Portland. And this is just the tip of the iceberg.

Mike Steele, who oversees DAWN in North America, has been personally monitoring the growth of house church networks throughout the USA and the world. He told me how he envisions this kind of church affecting every community:

I believe we will see a day when some cities will be "filled with the glory of the Lord as the waters cover the sea!" Division and petty jealousy will be replaced by a sacrificial call to serve the people of the city. Christians will be known for what they have done in humility rather than what they say in condemnation. There will be repentance, reconciliation and restoration in whole sections of the city. Communities will be filled with lighthouses, gatherings of believers who "are" the church and reach out to bless their neighbors and restore their neighborhoods. There will be a rapid multiplication of New Testament communities across this continent. We will see the "church" saturating neighborhoods and communities with the presence of Christ, in word and deed, on a sustained basis.

Many believers in non-western cultures have already caught the focus of the church being about "family." They are hotbeds for the growth of the kingdom as the church meets in homes.

House churches are springing up in America

Mike believes God is stirring the church in the West, to catch up with the non-western house church networks. He reports that many churches in America are beginning to see the church as a "life-style carried out in relationship in order to mentor, empower and release people for ministry." Here are just a few examples that he gives:

> House church networks are springing up around the country. Some have been going for a long time; others are just being birthed and some are only a few years old. The Foursquare church has a house church planting team in Canada. The Baptists in Texas have a network of five house churches in the Dallas area. Dallas has several folks spreading house churches across the city. There are house church networks emerging in Ames, Iowa, and Billings, Montana. One of my dear friends is leading a fellowship of home churches in Denver. They are currently meeting in four homes that soon will expand to nine. There is a house church network in Portland, Oregon, for over a decade. There are others meeting in Salem, Oregon. In Austin, Texas, there is a thriving house church network that is linking with house church networks in San Antonio and Dallas. In Houston, one of my good friends has a network of four house churches. They reach into the youth culture. There is a group from the San Francisco Bay area planting house churches in that city and a group of young people in Northern California planting 25 house churches.

"Churches in the home" networking with others in Virginia

My friend Tony Fitzgerald from Richmond, Virginia, oversees Church of the Nations, an apostolic movement with churches scattered throughout the world. An Australian, Tony has been a church planter in England, South Africa, and the USA and is a true father in the faith to church leaders in many nations. I ministered at a leadership conference at a church he oversees in Port Elizabeth, South Africa, which is touching thousands of people in their city and transitioning to a cell-based church. The weekend I was there, they were so excited because one cell group had recently seen twelve new believers come to faith in

Christ, and the people in the cell group were baptizing them the day I left the country.

Tony informed me that he is in a time of transition. Although he has seen the Lord work powerfully in the nations of the world and has seen churches established among the nations, he is transitioning to a new wineskin, a house church network in Richmond, Virginia. Tony believes the church needs to meet in the city both in the house and in celebration, relating to apostolic team life connected with the wider body of Christ. He said they do not call their house churches "house churches" because so many people in America associate unhealthy, negative churches with house churches. In these unhealthy house churches, believers have often chosen not to connect with the rest of the body of Christ in their communities. Tony's house church network is displaying a new attitude. They are learning to network together in their city, and they are calling their churches simply "church in the house."

House church network proposed in Canada

Bob Granholm, from Canada, is currently proposing the establishment of a new house church network in British Columbia. He is disturbed by the fact that 1.65 million Canadians express belief in the cardinal tenants of evangelical Christian faith, yet do not attend church. This finding is duplicated many times over throughout North America and the western world. Many believers are looking for authentic church life. They want to experience church from house to house just as Paul told the early Christians, "I...have taught you publicly and from house to house" (Acts 20:20).

House church network in Texas

Tony and Felicity Dale are both medical doctors from England who relocated to Austin, Texas, thirteen years ago. They had the privilege of being a part of a house church network in England more than twenty years ago. They are sensing the Lord is calling them back to their passion, ministering to people in their home as the Lord uses them to build His church from house to house. A few years ago, the pastors of their community church encouraged them to start a new church in their home that would multiply into a house church network. Their journey has begun. Not only have they started a house church network in Austin, they have started a new magazine entitled *House2House* that ministers to believers who have a heart for house churches and house church networks. You can visit their Web site at: www.house2house.tv.

House churches in India

In 1993, the Lord challenged Dr. Choudhrie, a well-known surgeon in India, to relinquish his professional career to establish the church in Madra Pradesh. The Lord has prospered this new work which started from scratch. Today, there have been 3,000 house churches established with an estimated 50,000 people. Dr. Choudhrie's vision is to plant a house church in each of the 17,000 villages of Madra Pradesh by the year 2007, and they are well on their way! One of the ladies they have trained started 50 house churches in a year!

The Lord is doing the same thing all over the world

About ten years after planting a new church, we received a phone call from Ralph Neighbour's office. I knew Ralph from his book, *Where Do We Go From Here?* that the Lord had used to open the hearts of thousands worldwide to the cell group movement. Since he was scheduled to speak in New Jersey, he asked to meet with me. Hank Rogers, our administrator, and I drove to New Jersey and met with Ralph during a break in his speaking engagement.

"Tell me your story," Ralph said. As I told him about our church starting with one cell group and growing to over 2,300 people all participating in cell groups, tears began to stream down his face. "The Lord is doing the same thing all over the world," Ralph exclaimed. "People who have never met, have never heard of one another, are using the same terminology because the Lord is doing the same thing through them in many parts of the world. This is truly the Lord."

As I travel week after week, I find the same being said of house church networks. They are springing up literally all over the world. They are using much of the same terminology, in spite of the fact they have never met one another. This is truly the hand of God.

A "house church" vs. "organized church" mentality

Not every house church will be a perfect example of a community of people in close-knit, interpersonal relationships. Relational Christianity in house churches can be messy.

Additionally, like any church, house churches can get off-track. If you have been turned off by those involved in house churches who have been exclusive, bitter, or proud, please do not "throw the baby out with the bath water." A group should be forewarned that when they take on a mentality that their group is best ("Us four, no more!"), they are on dangerous ground. We must guard against a "house church" versus an "organized church" mentality.

I have prayed with believers of house churches who have been hurt by believers from community churches and mega-churches. On the other hand, I have also prayed with believers from community churches and mega-churches who have been offended by believers involved in house churches. If any kind of church (community, mega- or house) becomes controlling or exclusive in its thinking, it has derailed. We are all a part of the worldwide body of Christ. There is only one church, and we must make every effort to walk in unity. Love always believes the best (1 Corinthians 13:5-6). The Lord will take us in our weakness and bring good out of us if we submit to Him.

Unity must be restored

"They will know we are Christians by our love." The words to a popular 1970s church camp song rings true in any day and age. Today more than ever, people are looking for a unified church—people who love each other and make an effort to reach out to those different from themselves. The world is attracted by Christians who truly love each other. Jesus required it of true disciples: "A new command I give you: Love one another. As I have loved you, so you must love one another. By this all men will know that you are my disciples, if you love one another" (John 13:34-35).

Jesus knew that the love and unity of His believers sent a compelling message to unbelievers. With this in mind, He prayed for all believers in John 17:20-23:

My prayer is not for them alone. I pray also for those who will believe in me through their message, that all of them may be one, Father, just as you are in me and I am in you. May they also be in us so that the world may believe that you have sent me. I have given them the glory that you gave me, that they may be one as we are one: I in them and you in me. May they be brought to complete unity to let the world know that you sent me and have loved them even as you have loved me.

Jesus does not pray for His followers to "become one," but rather that they may "be one." The present subjunctive used here in the Greek designates ongoing action: "continually be one," a oneness based on their common relationship to the Father and the Son, and on having the same basic attitude toward the world, the Word and the need to reach out to the lost.[5] As believers, we will "be one" if we continue to be in unity with God and each other. Unity breaks down barriers!

I believe the Lord is doing an awesome thing in our day. He is restoring the unity He prayed for in John 17:21: "That all of them may be one, Father, just as you are in me and I am in you. May they also be in us so that the world may believe that you have sent me." Walls that have divided denominations and churches for centuries are coming down throughout the world at an increasing rate. Pastors in the same town who never knew one another are now finding each other, praying together regularly, and supporting each other. This kind of church unity is exciting!

The regional church

Unity like this makes room for the regional church to emerge. What is the regional church? I believe it will be comprised of all types of churches—community churches, mega-churches, and house churches in a particular geographical area. These churches, of many different denominations, will work together to represent the church (the body of Christ) in a region.

In the New Testament, each church was identified by its geographical location—there were no denominations back then! The body of Christ met in house

The regional church includes the three kinds of churches in a geographical area

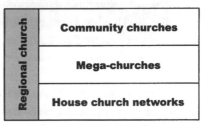

churches within a city, and they were unified by their specific city boundaries: the church of Antioch, the church of Corinth, the church of Jerusalem, the church of Smyrna. However, today, the church has been divided into many different denominations within one geographical area. Many times, such things as doctrinal interpretations and worship styles were the cause of these divisions in the body of Christ.

The regional church is not an attempt to do away with denominations and get back to separating believers on the basis of geographical distance exclusively. I believe we have to work with what we have today. This means that the local churches within a collective regional church will probably each maintain their denominational flavor, while working in a unified manner to more effectively share Christ in their geographical area. In short, I believe when unbelievers see the unity of churches in their community, they will be attracted to Christianity.

Fathers will unify to lead the regional church

Over the next years, I believe there will be an emergence of spiritual leaders from various backgrounds and denominations who will form teams of spiritual leadership to "father" this collective, regional church. These apostolic fathers will serve the church in towns, cities and regions to resource the body of Christ. They will not think only in terms of pastoring a church or churches, but will think and pray in terms of sensing a responsibility with other fellow servant-leaders throughout the body of Christ to pastor their region.

This initiative will not be contrary to their denomination's vision, but will bring wholeness. Although these "fathers of the region" will be concerned about unity, it will not be their focus. Their main focus will be on the Lord and on His mandate to reach the lost as the Lord brings in His harvest. Again, the regional church will include all the types of churches in a geographical location—the community churches, the megachurches, and the house church networks. All denominations and church movements operating in a region have a redemptive purpose to meet the needs of that particular region.

Churches in a region will honor each other

When LaVerne and I were married in 1971, we found we had two sets of relationships to pursue and maintain: those on her side of the family and those on mine. Both were important.

We need to maintain healthy relationships with the apostolic fathers of our church movement, and we also need to keep healthy relationships with the spiritual fathers of our region. When Ford Corporation runs a car through the assembly line at Detroit, the parts have been gathered from companies all over the world. God has brought together from around the world the unique mix of denominations and church families and has assembled them in your city. Each church and ministry is to be honored. As we walk together in unity in our region, the Lord will command a blessing.

When one studies the revivals found in church history, it is seen that unity among pastors and church leaders in a region is one of the most important prerequisites to revival in a region. Apostolic fathers serving towns, cities, and regions carry the mantle of unity that brings revival. There are apostolic fathers who serve in leadership over movements, and apostolic leaders who serve in leadership over regions. Some apostolic leaders serve in both areas of leadership. These spiritual fathers are not self-appointed, but recognized by the leadership of the church and ministries in the region they represent.

God is bringing people of various backgrounds and affiliations together in unity. God is using these divine connections to accomplish His purposes.

An example of regional church unity

I see this kind of unity beginning among the churches in our region of Lancaster County, in south central Pennsylvania. I am excited about a local regional Christian leadership group that has recently emerged and is in place to "empower the church in its many expressions throughout the region." Hundreds of leaders in our county are committed to working together as a leadership community regardless of their affiliation. They represent church leadership, ministry leadership, and Christians in leadership in the marketplace (areas of media, commerce, education and government). This regional group is not an organization to join, but an organized network of leaders devoted to relationships.

Through prayer and fasting, they have appointed 26 Christian leaders to work together on a council to oversee the Christian leadership community. Council members include Christian leaders from many types of churches, leaders in business, key ministry leaders and even a County Commissioner. Some are members of community churches, others members of mega-churches, while others are members of a new house church network but all are members of the body of Christ in our region.

The regional council has prayerfully chosen seven from among them to consider leading the council as an executive team. Presently, four of the seven have begun to serve while the other three are waiting for the Lord's timing to serve on the team. We asked one of the leaders of the four to serve as a team leader, and he is currently taking that responsibility.

The vision is to "see the church maturing in Christ, strategically serving together to revitalize the church, give a Christ-centered witness to each resident, and bring transformation to the way of life in this region." This regional team is committed to cooperate in establishing the kingdom of God in the home, neighborhood, community and marketplace. When the body of Christ joins in unity like this, we are bound to see results! This effort is an attempt to coordinate rather than control the work of God in our region. Cooperative efforts must always have this perspective.

I believe God calls Christians from community churches, megachurches, and house church networks to serve together as the regional church in every city in every nation. Together, we can reach the world!

Notes
[1] "Facts on Homeschooling" by the National Home Education Research Institute, www.homeschoolfaq.com
[2] "Home School," by John Cloud and Jodie Morse, *Time,* August 27, 2001, p. 47
[3] Wolfgang Simson, *Houses that Change the World,* (Cumbria, UK: OM Publishing, 2001), p. 94
[4] DAWN Report, "The Church Comes Home," August 1999, pp. 1-2
[5] *Full Life Study Bible,* NIV, (Grand Rapids, MI: Zondervan Publishing House) p.1621

The Chinese and
the Baptists are
Leading the Way

In this chapter, we will look at some major house church movements in today's world. Along with China, the Baptists with their Church Planting Movements have found amazing success.

China's house church movement

The revival in China today is considered the largest spiritual harvest since the book of Acts. The Cultural Revolution with its severe persecution of Christians only fueled the revival. Today, an estimated 25,000 Chinese are becoming Christians every day through various house church movements that have sprung up throughout their nation. There are over 80 million believers in these unregistered house churches in China.

In January 2001, I had the opportunity to minister to eighty of the key leaders of the underground church movements in China. It was life-changing for me. Meeting these humble men and women of God deeply moved me. I know one thing for sure: they taught me far more than I could teach them.

Ninety-five percent of these leaders, many of whom had traveled four days by train to get to the secluded leadership training seminar, had been imprisoned for their faith. One elderly leader had just been released four days before.

One precious man of God, who sat at our breakfast table, told us humbly that he gives leadership to 10 million believers meeting in house churches in the house church (network) he oversees. I sat in amazement! It was as if I was in another world. I met a group of women who oversee house church leaders, one of whom was responsible for 400,000 believers involved in a house church network. They told stories of being raped in prison, yet they stayed true to the Lord and continued to birth house churches as new people have come to Christ all over their nation.

I was asked to teach on the biblical truth of becoming spiritual fathers and mothers. After many of the sessions, these humble men and women of God stood, prayed and repented. It was such a humbling experience. They repented because they felt they were so caught up in the work of God, they were not focusing enough on the workers of God. This is a great lesson for all of us to learn. We can become so caught up in God's work, including the starting of new house churches, that we lose sight of our call from the Lord to be a spiritual father or mother to the next generation.

The Chinese church has gone "underground" in house churches out of necessity, but they are committed to following this biblical pattern, regardless of what happens politically. They cannot register their churches with the government, since to do so, would mean they could not teach their children about Christ in church settings until they were 18 years of age.

God has poured out His grace on the Chinese church. This "underground church" is probably experiencing the greatest move of God in history since Pentecost, and it is all happening in and through house churches. This is the most strategically organized church in the world, all meeting together in networked house churches.

Chinese vision to send traveling missionaries to start house churches

The Chinese church has a long-reaching vision to train 100,000 missionaries in their own country and send them out to take the Good News of Christ to the millions in spiritual darkness across Asia. The plan is called "Back to Jerusalem" and involves sending the missionaries west on a "mission journey" to several people groups as they make their way to Jerusalem.

Churches will be planted along the way as they take three main routes through the "final frontiers of the least evangelized nations in the world." The first two routes are meant to evangelize mostly through Muslim countries, and the third route will evangelize in the center of the Buddhist and Hindu world:

> The first missionaries are already on their way. Many more are preparing themselves for the Great Task, and will soon follow the others. They are learning different languages, for example Arabic and English. They are also being educated in learning the manners and culture of the countries they will enter.[1]

There has already been significant revival in Nepal, and in various parts of Vietnam and India. These churches serve as a base for the further planting of churches. "The Chinese know that it is of no avail to come to these countries with words only. They must come in power as well, the power of the Gospel—with signs and wonders to convince the people that there is a living and real God whom they can serve."[2]

Future strategy of the Chinese church

The Chinese house church movement has made a commitment to the Lord concerning how the church will exist even when they are freed from communism in the future. They have already made a decision that they will build no buildings. They want to keep their method of training and sending intact, and not focus on constructing buildings but on building people. They seek to accomplish this by (1) not allowing any pastor to stay in one place for a long period of time since this can create a dependency on leadership to do what all believers should be doing—evangelizing and planting new churches; (2) continue their commitment to build and model teamwork; (3) keep a tabernacle rather than a temple mentality. Like the Israelites in the Old Testament, they will move when the cloud moves.

I came home from China forever changed. May we all learn from their modeling of humility and desperation for God.

When I asked the Chinese leadership if the people in their house churches tithed, they said "yes." When I asked them if the house church pastors received support from the tithe, they smiled and informed me that only those individuals who are willing to be sent out as missionaries or apostolic leaders to other parts of China receive any financial support. This is also true of most house church leaders in North America. They either have a business or work at a job to support themselves and their families. They are "tent-makers" like Aquila and Priscilla who had a church in their home (Romans 16:3-5; 1 Corinthians 16:19). Only when they have the responsibility to oversee other house church leaders are leaders supported financially.

The Baptists have uncovered a secret: Church Planting Movements

About twelve years ago, the Southern Baptist Mission Board made a paradigm shift in the way they approached missions. They decided to plant churches the way they did in the book of Acts by training and releasing. They developed a Church Planting Movement (CPM) strategy and defined this movement as *a rapid and exponential increase of indigenous churches planting churches within a given people group or population segment.*

Encouraging church planting done by the churches themselves, led to numerous new church starts. In Latin America, church planters began by becoming spiritual fathers and mothers who trained and released their spiritual sons and daughters to become new house church planters. In 1989, in one Latin American area there were 129 churches. Nine years later, the number had grown to 1,918! These house church networks have grown exponentially. In 1989, in India, they started with 28 churches that grew to 2,000 in the same nine years. These results have been duplicated in Cambodia, a country with an infrastructure in shambles due to wars and dictatorships. In the same time, they grew from 6 to 194 churches. The majority of these churches are networked house churches.

A factor that fueled the growth of these house church networks in Latin America was the severe economic crisis in the early 1990's. Church members were prevented from traveling any long distances to their church buildings so they "moved their meetings into homes and found that growth greatly accelerated." [3]

In India, the Baptists implemented a plan to send out disciples two by two just as Jesus did in Luke 10. They found "men of peace" in targeted villages and moved in with them and began discipling their families. "As these initial converts came to faith, they led their families to the Lord, baptized them and forged them into the nucleus of new churches in each village." [4]

As the Baptist CPM unfolded in Cambodia, the momentum burned from within. "Local leaders expressed their own vision for planting churches in every district and within each ethnic community. As they acquired training and encouragement, the primary church planters were the church members themselves, rather than missionaries or professional church planters. The coordinator later observed that 'churches planted by other churches are reproducible, but those started by funded church planters are not (with few exceptions).'" [5]

Key factors for Church Planting Movement success

The Baptists claim there are several key components to CPM's. First, they reproduce rapidly. A CPM has rapid increases in new church starts. Second, there is a multiplicative increase. Multiplicative increase is only possible when new churches are being started by the churches themselves—rather than by professional church planters or missionaries. Third, they are indigenous churches. This means they are generated from within rather than from without. This is not to say that the gospel is able to spring up intuitively within a people group. The gospel nearly always enters a people group from the outside; this is the task of the missionary. However, in a church planting movement, the momentum quickly becomes indigenous, so that the initiative and drive of the movement comes from within the people group rather than from those outside.

One of the key elements of these CPM's is the house churches. They say, "The vast majority of the churches continue to be small, reproducible cell churches of 10-30 members meeting in homes or store-fronts." [6]

What about Baptist Church Planting Movements in the West?

It is a fact that the successful CPM's of the Baptist church are in largely non-western cultures. Here author of *Church Planting Movements*, David Garrison, speaks out about why he believes we have not seen huge movements in the western world yet:

One of the common characteristics that we've seen of church planting movements is persecution, and in many open democracies, you don't have that. Persecution often creates a climate of urgent need in response to Christ. This is one of the factors noted in why we don't see more CPM's in the West. One CPM that we did see was in Amsterdam among immigrants, refugees who came into the area. They were extremely responsive and began reproducing churches at a rapid clip.

There is an awful lot to commend house churches in the United States. There are quantifiable realities, such as the cost of church buildings, the exploding population, the increase in urbanization and the increasing cost of property in the cities. There is no way we can build enough church buildings. It becomes a question of stewardship. Can you justify putting 20-30 million dollars into building a church just so that you can add another 1,000 people to a church that already has a couple of thousand people? When we understand that people make up the church rather than church buildings, more and more people will come to the conclusion that we have to have new wineskins for the body of Christ.

I am concerned about the 80+ million unchurched Americans. I'm not convinced that our existing structures will draw them in. The house church movement has the potential to do that. It does not yet appear as it shall be. We are still in a transition stage. I'm excited to see what the models are that will emerge from this.[7]

I agree with Garrison's assessment of why church planting movements are so important in our western culture. It is in our best interests in North America to think in terms of starting CPM's, not just local house churches. If you have a vision from the Lord to plant a house church, go to your knees until you receive a vision to start or to help start a CPM. When Barnabas and Saul were sent out of the church in Antioch in Acts 13, they started a church planting movement. Acts 13, 14 and 15 tells the story of this new CPM that emerged from house to house nearly everywhere they went.

We need a spiritual rabbit plague

Wolfgang Simson says we need a "spiritual rabbit plague." I'm sure you know that elephants and rabbits have vastly different gestation periods and fertility capabilities. Rabbits multiply quickly while elephants produce their young less often. Both a rapid rabbit proliferation and slower elephant proliferation is needed to produce the results of carrying the gospel to all the earth.

I believe the rapid rabbit kind of reproduction will happen through the third kind of church—the house church networks. Because the house church model lends itself to quick reproduction of leaders, the numerical potential of the house church networks is enormous. Simson writes:

> As we all work together towards discipling the nations and filling the earth with the knowledge of the Lord like water covers the sea, we should all appreciate and acknowledge elephant-type structures and churches. God has blessed through them, is using them and will continue to use them. However, I am convinced that the bulk of the work of discipling whole nations is calling loud and clear for something beyond that, which I call a spiritual rabbit plague.

Elephants	Rabbits
fertile four times a year	practically continuously fertile
one baby per pregnancy	average of seven babies per pregnancy
22 month gestation period	1 month gestation period
sexual maturity: 18 years	sexual maturity: 4 months
grow in 3 years from 2 to 3	grow in 3 years from 2 to 476 million

With several million churches still needed to fill the earth, it's going to take both elephants and rabbits to get the job done![8]

Cell groups have opened the door for house churches to emerge

I've had the privilege of being involved in cell church ministry for more than 20 years. In fact, cell church is the only type of church structure in which I've had leadership experience. Today, churches of nearly all denominations are receiving a revelation from the Lord that the believers should be the ministers. So, I get the opportunity to train leaders in effective cell ministry throughout the nations.

Because of this, I am convinced that the most effective house church networks will be made up of cell-based house churches. Obviously, when a new house church begins, it starts as one cell group. But as it grows, wise house church leaders will train leaders within the group to lead small satellite cell groups as a part of their leadership training for future house church leadership. One house church could be comprised of several small cell groups. In addition to the house church meeting each week, two or three smaller cells of believers would also meet for breakfast or at another time to pray and be accountable with their Christian lives.

The cell movement has been used by the Lord to open up the church at large to the truths of the priesthood of every believer. It has also opened the door for healthy house church networks to emerge. Many cell churches will birth house churches out of their churches in the coming years. I spoke with a pastor of a cell church in Indiana who recently released a new house church from his church with a vision to start a house church network. The leadership of the house church will continue to look to the senior pastor and the elders of the sending church for oversight as they enter into this holy experiment.

Recently, I was in England training Anglican vicars in cell-based ministry. The Lord is doing some amazing things within the organized church of England. Many are realizing that people "learn by doing" and a most effective way to learn to minister is through small groups. However, as I talked to the younger generation, many are searching for something beyond current church experience. When I spoke about house church networks, they seemed to come alive with fresh vision for their future.

Notes

1 Haavald Slaatten, *The Heavenly Man*, (Ontario, Canda: Guardian Books, 2000), p. 128
2 Ibid., p. 129
3 David Garrison, *Church Planting Movements*, (Richmond, VA: International Mission Board of the Southern Baptist Convention, 1999) p. 14
4 Ibid., p. 23
5 Ibid., p. 30
6 Ibid., p. 35
7 *House2House Magazine*, "A Telephone Interview with David Garrison," Issue 2, p. 9
8 Wolfgang Simson, *Houses that Change the World*, (Cumbria, UK: OM Publishing, 2001), p. 106

6

The Next Generation Speaks Out

A few months ago, I spoke at a Bible school sponsored by a thriving mega-church in the United States. After the class was completed, a young man in his mid-twenties came up to me and opened his heart. "I have been a staff member of this church for the past few years. I have not told anyone yet, but I am planning to quit and move on to something else. I can't take it anymore. This is a great church, and I love the leaders and the other staff. But they are too busy. If just one of them gave me only one hour a month to sit down with me for breakfast and hear my heart, I would stay. What I really want is a father. I just do not feel I fit in here. Therefore, I am going to leave. I need to find a place I fit. Even though good things are happening here, it is just not me. I must take a step of faith and find my way. There has to be more."

I hear this same heart cry repeatedly from one end of our nation to the other. The value system of Generation X is much different from the value system I grew up with. I was a part of the industrial age. Generation X is a part of the information age, and it has its own value system. Older adults must recognize the tremendous changes that have taken place and make some adjustments accordingly if they hope to have significant involvement with the younger generation.

Wolfgang Fernandez, director of International Ministries for DAWN Ministries, says we need a new model of church for this young generation: "I think we need a new model, a new shape of church, and a new vision of what church is. This will mean defining a new vision for what we mean by church planting. If church continues to look like a building with a program and a congregational format for all the people…it appears that you are going to have to buy a building or sell one first so that you can bring the people together…this won't work in our youth culture. We need a new model of church in youth culture." [1]

Let's listen to the voice of the next generation and hear their hearts' cry. On my travels, I have found the young people of Generation X value four basic things. Amazingly, house church networks are the perfect wineskin for each of these values to be realized and experienced.

The four basic values of the next generation

What do Generation Xers look for in a church? The four top things I hear repeatedly from this generation is that they are looking for relationship, authenticity, the freedom to be creative and intergenerational connection.

Relationship Young people just want others with whom they can connect. They love to "hang out" with friends. They really value their relationships.

Authenticity They are tired of the plastic, smiling Christianity, where things look good on the surface, but underneath it isn't real. They are looking for people who are real who live out their Christianity authentically every day. If they blow it, they say so, receive forgiveness and move on.

Freedom to be creative They want the freedom to express Christianity in a way that is unique to them. They say, "The kind of church I'm involved with may look different from other churches. I may be involved with one particular sector of society because that is where God has called me."

Intergenerational connection I hear them say again and again, "I don't want to do it myself. I want fathers and mothers in the Lord who will encourage me, help me avoid pitfalls, and release me to fulfill my destiny in God."

The house church network gives the opportunity to experience these four values!

The next generation speaks out

During the past three and a half years, a group of young men and women started a Bible Study in our county. This weekly Bible Study now has grown to 1,000 young people coming together every Tuesday evening. Even the secular press in our community has taken notice. A few months ago, in our evening paper, there was a front-page feature of the Tuesday Bible Study. Literally thousands of youth from our region have been touched by the Lord through this weekly gathering simply known as "TBS." Will Stolzfus, one of the leaders of TBS, was on the leadership team of TBS from the beginning. He was only 19 years old when TBS started. Today he is 22. I have asked Will to share in this chapter what his generation is looking for in the church:

> As I ponder the question of what the younger generation is looking for in the church, the question itself strikes me. The reality is that there are countless young people who are looking for answers and truth, but many of them are not looking to the church for the answers. In fact, many of them actually blame the church for problems in their lives. While many of their perspectives are skewed by bitterness and disappointment, we must hear what they are saying if we want to reach them with the gospel.
>
> Although I love and support the churches that call on the name of Jesus, I have met many people who don't. These people are both Christians and non-Christians.

Authenticity

> Recently I was talking to a friend of mine who had just had a conversation with a person that had grown up in the church, but currently wants nothing to do with Christianity. My friend asked this person what problems he had with Christianity, and the reply was he had a problem with the people who "claim" to be Christians. My friend then asked what he disagreed with in Jesus' teachings. His answer was simple. It wasn't a matter of being upset at Jesus but the people who represented Him.
>
> This story relates well with what I have heard from a great number of people from my generation. What young people are looking for today is something that is "real," something that is

much more than words. There is a strong desire to see the reality of truth working itself out in people's lives. To put it simply: there is a strong distaste for empty religion, but real hunger to have an authentic spiritual encounter. What turns so many people away from Jesus is when we call on His name and talk about what He has done for us, but our lives do not reflect what comes from our mouths. I have been convicted on numerous occasions for not living my life in accordance with the things that I believe.

Often, we can learn a lot from non-Christians. Many times, they are more open and honest with each other than Christians are. In talking to a friend of mine who got saved in the past two years, and who still spends time with many non-Christians, he said that one of the things that he enjoys about his unchurched friends is how they will hang out with each other and just spend time together and be open about their lives. As I look at my life, I see that for the most part, I am caught up with doing, doing, doing, and in my busyness, I miss simple relationship building. What the world wants to see from us, particularly young people, is that we are real, open and honest.

Relationship

Another thing that young people are looking for in the church is real relationship and connection with people. Recently a few friends of mine had the opportunity to lead several people to Jesus. How did it happen? They just began to spend time with the pre-Christians. It didn't happen in church or at a church function. They just got together and hung out. Through their times together, they were able to share Jesus. Because the Christian young people had built a relationship with them, the unbelievers came to Christ. As new believers, they are now growing and being discipled by my friends, through natural relationships.

Creativity

Young people of today also have a strong desire to see creativity within the church. God has given us creative minds and hearts. Sadly enough, even when we desire to see creativity, our current structures make it hard to release it. We have a desire, as well we should, to keep things orderly and organized. The bigger our groups get, the harder it is to be creative and flexible. While I know that I have my own tastes and preferences, many people see things entirely differently than I do. We must have avenues for people to express who they are in church settings. The main thing we must guard against when creating room for flexibility and creativity is that we do not compromise biblical truth in doing so.

Intergeneration connection

Due to the staggering number of young people (both inside and outside of the church) who do not have true fathers and mothers in their lives, there is a strong desire within the young people of today to connect with those who are older. It has been said by many people that the younger generations of today are fatherless and motherless generations. The enemy has ravaged our nation with this breakdown of family life, and it has left many feeling hopeless, lost and insecure. God is using that void, however, to turn the hearts of the fathers and mothers to the children and the hearts of the children to fathers and mothers. Many will come into the kingdom because of being connected to spiritual fathers and mothers within.

In conclusion, God is at work all over the world. He is preparing us for a mighty harvest of souls. In this preparation process, there are changes that He is bringing to the structure of His body. He is not removing the older wineskins, but He is completing them by bringing new wineskins alongside of them to work in the harvest together.

Let's empower our young people!

If you are a pastor or a Christian leader, let me take a moment and speak with you. Now is the time for the generations to come together to build His kingdom! We must commission this next generation to establish their own new churches. We must not hold them back. Let's empower these young people. And then rejoice with them when they reproduce!

Many of the younger generation in our churches are sensing a desire to experience something new. They are no longer satisfied with the church structure of their present and prior experience. We need to release them to build their own structures and reproduce. A few years ago, Rick Joyner from Charlotte, North Carolina, told a group of pastors in our city: "Pastors sometimes don't like having young stallions in their churches. They seem to cause too many problems. But only young stallions can reproduce. Resist the temptation to "fix" them so they cannot reproduce!"

A group of 18 to 35 year olds recently shared with me: "We like our churches and our pastors, but our present churches are not something we want to give our lives for. We lead cell groups, youth groups and serve in the church, but we do not want to do this our whole lives. God is calling us to something new—new kinds of churches. We are not even sure what it will look like, but we want the opportunity to try. We are not rebellious. We want the blessing of the leaders of our churches. We respect and honor them. But we want to build our own house. There are things the Lord has placed inside of us that we desire to see become reality. It is good to have a room within our father's house, but we have a God-given desire to build a new home."

I understood completely. I remembered how I felt when I was in my 20's and the Lord called me to start a new church—a new wineskin. During the early 1980s, when I was a new pastor, new churches were springing up everywhere in our area. The majority of the leaders were in their twenties, many in their early twenties. Barry Wissler, who pastors Ephrata Community Church in our region and oversees Harvest-Net, a new apostolic network of churches, was only twenty years of age when he planted a new church. I was in my late twenties. A word to us oldsters: let's not forget where we came from!

The reality is this: new wineskins eventually get old. I believe God often places a burden in the younger generation to pioneer new churches, but they have a different vision for a different era and a different generation. The younger generations come into the kingdom looking for reality—not religious structures. They want relationships—not outdated church programs. Let's help them start the new church structures that fit the needs of their generation.

Notes
[1] *Religion Today*, "Look Out, Here Comes the Gen-X Church," January 2001

7
The Role of Spiritual Fathers and Mothers

A major aspect of house church ministry is preparing and training future spiritual fathers and mothers and then releasing them to reproduce themselves. I will never forget the experience of having our first baby. I had faithfully attended prenatal classes with LaVerne where I learned how to coach, but when the contractions started, reality hit me. We were going to have a baby! I just didn't feel like I was ready. I was too young. We had never done this before. I felt like telling LaVerne, "Couldn't you just put it on hold for a few months until we are ready?" But waiting was not an option. She was going to give birth, and our baby girl was to be born now whether I felt ready or not.

It really felt strange being a "papa." We had never been down this road before. Somehow, with the faithful advice of trusted family and friends, it all worked out.

That was twenty-six years ago. When this "baby" girl got married, we gave her away. She had gone from being a baby, to a teenager, to an adult. Now, she was ready to go and parent the next generation. As of this writing, she has given birth to two children. These grandchildren of ours will go on to be parents themselves, and another generation will be born!

When it comes to spiritual parenting, many potential spiritual parents go through the same emotions and fears. "How could God ever use me to be a spiritual parent? What if I can't do it properly? Am I really ready for this?" However, as they are encouraged to take a step of faith and obedience, they begin to experience the joy of becoming a spiritual father or mother. They have the satisfaction of training and releasing others for eternity.

Only a dysfunctional parent will try to hang on to his children and use them to fulfill his own vision. Healthy parents expect their children to leave their home to start their own families. Healthy spiritual parents must think the same way. This generation of Christian leaders are called to "give away" many of the believers in their churches to start their own spiritual families—new house churches.

According to the Bible, there are three different types of people in our churches: spiritual children, young men and fathers. 1 John 2:12-13 tells us, "I write to you, dear children, because your sins have been forgiven on account of his name. I write to you, fathers, because you have known him who is from the beginning. I write to you, young men, because you have overcome the evil one..." Let's take a look at these three types of people and how they can be prepared and trained to become spiritual parents.

1. Spiritual children

There are many spiritual babies (new Christians) in the church to-day, with few spiritual fathers and mothers available to disciple them. Nevertheless, the larger problem seems to be the many "spiritual baby Christians" who never grew up—many of whom are unaware they are still infants. Their spiritual chronological age may be twenty, thirty, forty or fifty years old, but they remain on "the milk." They make a fuss when they don't get their own way, complain about not being fed and have not yet taken spiritual responsibility to train the next generation.

2. Spiritual young men and women

Spiritual young men, according to the Bible, have the Word of God abiding in them and have overcome the wicked one. They have learned to feed on the Word for themselves in order to overcome the devil, but they have not yet become spiritual fathers.

When I was a child, I thought my father knew everything. When I became an adolescent, I felt there were a few things he didn't know. By the time I was in my mid teens, in my youthful arrogance I just figured my father was still living in the stone ages. However, when I became a father, I was amazed at how much my father had learned during the past few years! In reality, by becoming a father, my perspective changed. In the same way, having spiritual children also changes our perspective.

3. Spiritual fathers and mothers

One of the greatest catalysts to maturity as a Christian is to become a spiritual father or mother. Many of the problems that surface in churches today are the product of: (1) spiritual young men and women who are full of the Word of God but have not had the experience of becoming spiritual parents, and (2) church leaders who have not released and encouraged the spiritual young men and women within their church to have their own spiritual children. House churches solve these training and leadership issues because they develop spiritual fathers and mothers in-house in a natural, family-like setting.

Reproducing ourselves

We must think in terms of our spiritual children starting their own house churches in the future. Without raising up spiritual fathers and mothers today, we are in danger of losing the next generation. If we do not believe we have the grace to start a church planting movement, then we should ask the Lord to join us to a church planting movement so we can be productive.

My extended family gathers every year for a reunion—aunts, uncles, brothers, sisters, cousins, nephews, and nieces who are all connected to the Kreider family. When my grandparents were alive, I noticed how they seemed to look at each other with a twinkle in their eyes at these family gatherings. They knew we were all there because of them, and it gave them deep satisfaction to see their posterity.

The Lord wants to see spiritual families continually reproducing in each generation down through the ages. He has a generational perspective, and we must too. God is mentioned as the God of Abraham, Isaac and Jacob in the Old Testament. His very name shows a generational connection.

In the New Testament, Paul, the apostle, was thinking in terms of four generations when he called Timothy his son and exhorted him to find faithful men to whom he can impart what Paul taught him: "And the things you [second generation] have heard me [first generation] say in the presence of many witnesses entrust to reliable men [third generation] who will also be qualified to teach others [fourth generation]" (2 Timothy 2:2).

Paul was thinking about his spiritual posterity and speaking as a spiritual father to his spiritual son Timothy who would give him spiritual grandchildren and great grandchildren. The entire Bible was written from a family perspective. It was natural for Paul to think in terms of spiritual posterity because that is how biblical society was set up and the way God intended it to be.

Birthing a spiritual lineage

In Genesis 15:1, when God spoke to Abraham about a promised spiritual seed, He said, "Do not be afraid, Abram. I am your shield, your very great reward." When God gives us a spiritual revelation to be spiritual parents, we need not be afraid. We may make mistakes or sometimes get hurt by people we are helping, but we have a shield to protect us. God will be our great reward.

Abraham was ninety-nine years old when God gave him the promise that he would be the "father of many nations" (Genesis 17:4). This covenant also promised that his descendants would be "as numerous as the stars in the sky" (Genesis 26:4).

True, this covenant is speaking about the covenant between God and Abraham and the Jewish people. But Galatians 3:29 says that those who belong to Christ are "Abraham's seed, and heirs according to the promise."

Therefore, as believers, God wants to birth in us "nations," too. These "nations" or groups of people, who come to know God because of our influence, will be our spiritual lineage—they are our posterity in God's kingdom. We have been promised it because we are children of promise. Our God desires to give us a spiritual posterity.

Our inheritance of spiritual children

This promise of spiritual children is for every Christian! God has placed us here on earth because He has called us to become spiritual fathers and mothers in our generation. With this comes the expectation that our spiritual children will have spiritual children and continue to produce more children into infinity.

Our inheritance will be the spiritual children that we can some day present to Jesus Christ. No matter what we do—whether we are a homemaker, a student, a worker in a factory, a pastor of a church, or the head of a large corporation—we have the divine blessing and responsibility to birth spiritual children, who will produce grandchildren and great grandchildren. We are all called to impart to others the rich inheritance that God has promised.

I like how Abraham responded when the Lord showed him the stars in the sky and promised him descendants as numerous as the stars: "Abram believed the Lord..." (Genesis 15:6). What did he believe the Lord for? His inheritance! We, too, need to "believe the Lord" for many spiritual children. We can trust God to do it. It may not happen overnight, but it will happen when we trust in God's faithfulness. We are promised an inheritance of spiritual children. God *wants* to give us an inheritance of spiritual children, and He will do it through the generations. He is a God who has a heart for families and is concerned about the generations to come.

Healthy families will multiply

The Lord wants us to be fruitful and multiply (Genesis 1:28). Our God is a God of multiplication. Multiplication is a fact of nature. As a farm boy, I once counted the kernels on a healthy stalk of corn and found there to be 1,200 kernels in the first generation. Do you know that by the next generation there will be one million, four hundred forty thousand kernels of corn?

In the same way, healthy cells in the body multiply and result in the body growing. A living cell is in a state of constant activity.

The church in the book of Acts multiplied rapidly because they understood the value of believers meeting in homes in spiritual family relationships. They functioned in close relationship with each other. This healthy activity and interdependence resulted in healthy growth for the early church.

As the Lord restores spiritual family life into His kingdom today, the church in our generation will also multiply rapidly. We must be ready. We must properly train and prepare spiritual parents, sons and daughters so that Christ may be formed in them.

Paul was longing to see his spiritual children in Thessalonica and says in 1 Thessalonians 2:19-20: "For what is our hope, our joy, or the crown in which we will glory in the presence of our Lord Jesus when he comes? Is it not you? Indeed, you are our glory and joy." His spiritual children were his glory and joy—his inheritance! Paul rejoiced like a winner receiving a garland of victory (crown) at the games when he thought of his spiritual children and grandchildren whom he would present to Christ.

I carry photos of my children and grandchildren with me when I travel. They are my joy and my posterity! When I look at them, I know I had a part in their being on this earth. Our spiritual sons, daughters and grandchildren are our spiritual posterity.

A spiritual legacy

I mention in my book *The Cry for Spiritual Fathers and Mothers* that a few years ago I was in Barbados training church leaders and believers on the subject of spiritual parenting and cell group ministry. The day I was to leave to come back to the USA, Bill Landis, a missionary who leads *Youth With A Mission's* Caribbean ministry, asked me to his home before going to the airport. Bill and his family, along with a team of leaders, spend their time training and equipping Christians to become spiritual leaders in the Caribbean. On this visit to Barbados, Bill told me some interesting history of this tiny island nation.

He explained that, years ago many in Barbados came as slaves to the island from West Africa including from the nation of Gambia. Now, after receiving Christ and being trained as missionaries, Barbadians were being sent to their ancestral country of Gambia to lead Muslim Gambians to Christ. With a common heritage, it was the ideal match. Then he said something that moved me deeply, "Larry, do you realize the people being reached in Gambia are a part of your spiritual heritage? You were one of my spiritual fathers."

As I sat on the plane returning to the United States, I was dumbfounded at the significance of Bill's words. Years ago, long before I was a pastor or a writer or a church leader, I was a young chicken farmer who led a Bible study of young people. During this time, I had become one of Bill's spiritual fathers.

Bill was now a spiritual father to those he had discipled in Barbados; and the Barbadian Christians who were now going to Africa and leading Gambians to Christ were like my spiritual great-grandchildren! Generations to come would receive God's promises because a chicken farmer had been obedient to God's call to disciple a bunch of teenagers more than twenty years ago. Yes, this was part of my spiritual legacy. As I pondered this reality, I was deeply moved by the Lord. It was as if I was the recipient of a large inheritance!

A sweeping revival is just around the corner. God's people need to be alert to accommodate the great harvest this will bring into the kingdom of God. Spiritual parents will need to be ready to obey His call and take these young Christians under their wings. God has called us to be spiritual parents. The Lord wants to give us a spiritual legacy. We may not feel ready; in fact, we may feel unprepared. Nevertheless, God's call remains on our lives.

Restoring the New Testament pattern

Although for the past 1700 years much of the church of Jesus Christ has strayed from the truth of relational restoration between fathers and sons, the Lord is breathing a fresh word to His people in our generation. Rather than having the focus on meetings and buildings which promote *programs* to encourage the spiritual growth of believers, He is calling us back to be His *family* and return to the New Testament truth of building families.

Many believers are meeting house to house in small groups throughout the world because the Lord is restoring this sense of family to the body of Christ. Christians are again beginning to relive the book of Acts. They are seeing the importance of empowering and parenting the next generation.

Parachurch organizations have understood this truth for years. Organizations like the *Navigators, Campus Crusade For Christ,* and *Youth With a Mission* applied Ephesians 4:16 in their ministry operations and found that if everyone is trained, the body of Christ will expand and grow: "From him the whole body, joined and held together by every supporting ligament, grows and builds itself up in love, as each part does its work." The body of Christ is meant to intricately fit together like the human body. When all members are working, the body of Christ will be healthy and grow.

Jesus wants His church to be restored to the New Testament pattern of family life. He ministered to the multitudes but focused on a few. These disciples changed the world!

I believe we are living in the days of preparation and restoration. God is preparing us for the job He has for us to do. We are pressing on

"...to take hold of that for which Christ Jesus took hold of me [us]" (Philippians 3:12). As we press on and determine to follow the pattern Jesus has set before us, He promises times of refreshing and restoration: "...that times of refreshing may come from the Lord...until the time comes for God to restore everything..." (Acts 3:19,21).

Thirsting for new wine

I believe the Lord is preparing to pour out His Spirit and bring revival to the church in these last days. There will be a greater awakening to the things of God in our communities, and many will be drawn into the kingdom of God. When the Lord pours out this new wine, we must have the new wineskins prepared or we will lose the harvest. The new wineskins (church structures) of the early church were simplistic: people met from house to house. I believe our Lord's strategy to prepare for the harvest is still the same—He wants to use common ordinary believers who have encountered an extraordinary God to meet together as spiritual families from house to house to disciple and train, preparing for the harvest.

Many Christians today are thirsting for this great influx of new wine—new believers pouring into His kingdom. God is placing a desire within spiritual fathers and mothers to welcome these believers into the kingdom and then train them as spiritual sons and daughters. Small groups of believers meeting in homes provide an ideal structure for this kind of training. The house church is meant to be a spiritual family with the leaders and other spiritual moms and dads in the group taking responsibility to train the spiritual children. House churches develop and produce mature Christians in a family-like setting.

Structure without relationships equals boredom

Although house churches and house church networks are wonderful wineskins for spiritual parenting, these house churches in themselves are not the answer. Plainly stated, *it is not the structure itself that is significant, but the relationships occurring within its perimeters*. If the people in the house churches do not practice spiritual parenting, they can find their groups quickly becoming as boring and as lifeless as any other structure. The life comes from the active father-son and mother-daughter relationships taking place within the house church network.

How do we become spiritual fathers or mothers?

Paul, the apostle, told the Corinthian church that they desperately needed fathers:

> Even though you have ten thousand guardians in Christ, you do not have many fathers; for in Christ Jesus I became your father through the gospel. Therefore I urge you, to imitate me (1 Corinthians 4:15-16).

So how does a young man or woman become a spiritual parent? The only way for a young man or woman to become a spiritual parent is to have children, either by adoption (becoming a spiritual father or mother to someone who is already a believer but needs to be discipled) or by natural birth (becoming a spiritual father or mother to someone you have personally led to Christ) and committing yourself to helping them grow. Paul became a spiritual father to Onesimus through "natural birth," leading him to Christ in prison (Philemon 10). Paul became a spiritual father to Timothy through "adoption" after meeting him in Ephesus (Acts 16:1-4).

The house church and cell group provides an ideal opportunity for everyone to experience a spiritual family and eventually become spiritual parents themselves. The purpose for house church multiplication and cell multiplication is to give the opportunity for new parents to take responsibility to start a new spiritual family (house church or cell group).

A spiritual father defined

Before we can ever be spiritual fathers or mothers, we must first check our motives. Spiritual fathering is a "behind the scenes" task. Probably no one will pat us on the back and say, "What a good job you are doing: keep up the good work." Why? Because being a father is not something we *do*, as much as it is something we *are*. I do not have to tell people that I'm a father. They know it when they see my son and daughters at my side.

Scripture warns us about giving ourselves an impressive title in an effort to try to gain the honor and respect of others: "Do not call anyone on earth your father; for One is your Father, He who is in heaven...But he who is greatest among you shall be your servant" (Matthew 23:9,11). A spiritual father is always a servant first. No one can ever take the place of our heavenly Father. Spiritual fathers point their spiritual children to their heavenly Father.

Paul, the apostle, called himself a father several times in scripture, but he uses the word "father" to denote, "not *authority*, but *affection*: therefore he calls them not his *obliged*, but his *beloved*, sons" (see 1 Corinthians 4:14).[1] The measure of greatness of a spiritual father is his level of servanthood and love, not his position.

Spiritual fathers and mothers could also be called *mentors*. The term *mentor* comes from Greek mythology where Odysseus asked his friend, Mentor, to look after his son while he went on a long journey. A spiritual mentor recognizes that people need to be developed through a caring and empathetic approach to teach them how to grow in Christ.

Simply stated, my favorite definition of a spiritual father would be: *A spiritual father/mother helps a spiritual son/daughter reach his God-given potential.* It is that uncomplicated and yet profound. Bobb Biehl says it this way: "Mentoring is more 'how can I help you?' than 'what should I teach you?'" [2]

More than twenty-five years ago, LaVerne and I, and a team of young people began to develop Paul-Timothy relationships with new Christians. I would meet with a few young men each week for Bible study and prayer and would try to answer their questions about life. LaVerne did the same with young women. Watching them grow from spiritual babies, to young men and women, to spiritual parents has brought great joy to our lives. It also caused great growth in our personal spiritual lives.

There is a tremendous need for spiritual parents in the church today. I can still hear the desperation in the voice of a dynamic young leader in New Zealand who opened his heart to me a few years ago. "I need a father," he stated. "Where are the spiritual fathers today?" Jesus took twelve men and became a spiritual father to them for three and a half years. He knew that Christianity was caught not just taught. He ministered to the multitudes, but most of His time was spent with these few men. His disciples changed the world. By our Lord's example, we can do the same.

You can be a spiritual parent!

Perhaps you feel you have already tried to be a spiritual parent but failed. Trust God for grace to start again. Someone once asked Mother

Teresa what she did when she got discouraged because she did not see immediate results. "God does not demand that I be successful," she said, "God demands that I be faithful. When facing God, results are not important. Faithfulness is what is important." [3]

Maybe you never had a spiritual father or mother. You can give someone else something you never had by being his or her spiritual parent. You do not need to be perfect, just faithful and obedient. If you and I wait until we think we are ready to be perfect parents, it will never happen.

Are you expecting the believers in your cell group or house church to become spiritual fathers or mothers? If not, you need to change your way of thinking. Many will become future cell leaders, elders, church planters and apostolic leaders as they fulfill their roles as spiritual parents. In the cell groups and house churches, they can experience "on the job training." In house church networks, cell leaders are called by the Lord to become spiritual parents to believers in cell groups within the house church while elders and pastors become spiritual parents to cell leaders. Apostolic leaders become spiritual parents to elders and pastors who lead house churches. The training occurs by participation and through modeling.

Notes

[1] *Matthew Henry's Commentary in One Volume*, (Grand Rapids, Michigan: Zondervan, 1960), p. 119

[2] Bobb Biehl, *Mentoring*, (Nashville, Tennessee: Broadman & Holman Publishers, 1996), p. 19

[3] *Mother Teresa In My Own Words*, Compiled by Jose Luis Gonzalez-Balado, (Random House, 1996), p. 40

Let's Get Back
to the Basics

Statistics are dismal concerning the contemporary church. They show the church in America losing its relevance in today's diverse and pluralistic world. Let's look at some sobering facts:

Churches lose an estimated 2,765,000 people each year to nominalism and secularism. Between 3,500 to 4,000 churches close their doors for the last time each year while 1,100 to 1,500 churches are started each year.[1]

The American church loses 72.11 churches per week or 10.27 per day and gains 24.03 per week or 3.42 per day.[2]

During the last ten years, the combined communicant membership of all Protestant denominations has declined by 9.5% (4,498,242), while the national population has increased by 11% (24,153,000).[3]

"No county in the U.S. has a higher percentage of churched people than it did 10 years ago." [4]

The USA ranks third behind China and India in the number of unsaved people. While America is the number one nation in sending out missionaries to other countries, we are now second to Brazil in the number of missionaries received. Half of all churches last year did not add one new member through "conversion growth." Evangelical churches have failed to gain an additional two percent of the American population in the past fifty years. In other words, we are not even reaching our own children.[5]

"Churches that reach the unchurched are highly intentional, and they understand the culture. A large element of being culturally aware is understanding the generation born between 1977-1994. Research indicates that only 4 percent of this group are Christians. By comparison, 65 percent of the generation born before 1946 are Christians. If there is one area where we are culturally unaware, it is this generation. This is the most unchurched generation in America." [6]

Rather than gaining ground, the contemporary church, especially in America, is sinking fast. We really need new wineskins to help revitalize today's church. It reminds me of a story I once heard about a rescue operation at sea. A boat had capsized and two men were floundering in the water until a helicopter dropped a rope to save them. Grabbing onto the rope would allow them to be pulled to safety, but it involved risk. Things could go wrong. The men, of course, took the risk because they did not have other options at that point! This is not to say house churches are the only options to save the church today! However, like the men in the water, the church of today should not be afraid of grabbing onto the rope. Yes, there are still challenges and chances we take as we enter into this uncharted territory of house churches and house church networks. But can we afford not to take hold of that rope?

I believe the new wineskins of house church networks will be a way of giving new life to the church. We must get back to the basics of seeing all the saints doing the work of ministry. Ordinary believers must be given the chance to allow God to do extraordinary things through them.

The book of Acts church was radical!

Compare our present-day church statistics to the book of Acts. In the early church, literally hundreds of believers opened up their homes to experience dynamic church life as thousands came to Christ. In the span of one day, Acts 2:41 tells us, about three thousand souls were added to the church!

How could the 120 disciples in the upper room possibly have taken care of 3,000 new believers? Part of their secret is found in Acts 2:46-47 (NKJ):

> So continuing daily with one accord in the temple, and breaking bread from **house to house,** they ate their food with gladness and simplicity of heart, praising God and having favor with all the people. And the Lord added to the church daily those who were being saved.

God's people met in small groups in homes: "They devoted themselves to the apostles' teaching and to the fellowship, to the breaking of bread and to prayer" (Acts 2:42). They began to minister to one another and to the unsaved on an individual basis, and the Lord kept adding to the church daily! In Acts 20:20, the apostle Paul declares to members of the church at Ephesus that, "You know that I have not hesitated to preach anything that would be helpful to you but have taught you publicly and from house to house."

The letter that Paul wrote to the Christians in Rome was written to believers in Jesus Christ who met in peoples' homes. In his letter to the Romans, Paul indicates that one of these groups met in the home of Priscilla and Aquila:

> Greet Priscilla and Aquila, my fellow workers in Christ Jesus. They risked their lives for me. Not only I but all the churches of the Gentiles are grateful to them. Greet also *the church that meets at their house* (Romans 16:3-5).

Paul also sent his greetings to the household of Aristobulus and the household of Narcissus (Romans 16:10-11). When Paul wrote to his friend Philemon, he expressed his greetings to the church in his house:

> To Philemon our dear friend and fellow worker, to Apphia our sister, to Archippus our fellow soldier and to the church that meets in your home (Philemon 1:2).

Periodically, down through the ages, the church has lost the New Testament component of meeting in small groups in the homes of individual believers and has placed an emphasis on the church as it meets in large buildings. James Rutz, an advocate of starting house churches, says:

> It was in 323 AD, almost three hundred years after the birth of the church, that Christians first met in something we now call a "church building." For all three hundred years before that, the church met in living rooms!
>
> Constantine built these assembly buildings for Christians not only in Constantinople, but also in Rome, Jerusalem, and in many parts of Italy, all between 323 and 327! This then triggered a massive "church building" fad in large cities all over the Empire.[7]

Temple ministry is beneficial for corporate worship, teaching and celebration, but the Lord wants us to get back to seeing the church as *people*, not as a place where people meet. Our homes, places of business, schools, and other circles of contact provide excellent places for the church to meet as we infiltrate our spheres of influence with the gospel of Jesus Christ.

What was the early church really like?

T.L. Osborne, in his book, *Soul-winning, Out Where the Sinners Are,* tells the story of a possible conversation with Aquila in Ephesus, from the book of Acts:

"Good evening, Aquila. We understand you're a member of the church here. Could we come in and visit for a while?"

"Certainly. Come in."

"If you don't mind, we would like for you to tell us about the way the churches here in Asia Minor carry on their soul-winning program. We read that you have been a member of a church in Corinth and Rome, as well as this one here in Ephesus. You should be very qualified to tell us about evangelism in the New Testament church. If you don't mind, we'd like to visit your church while we're here."

"Sit down, you're already in the church. It meets in my home.

You don't have a church building?"

"What's a church building? No, I guess we don't."

"Tell me Aquila, what is your church doing to evangelize Ephesus? What are you doing to reach the city with the gospel?"

"Oh, we already evangelized Ephesus. Every person in the city clearly understands the Gospel...We just visited every home in the city. That's the way the church in Jerusalem first evangelized that city (Acts 5:42). The disciples there evangelized the entire city of Jerusalem in a very short time. All the other churches in Asia Minor have followed that example." [8]

The church of today should follow the example of the early church. Today's church has tried to reach people for Christ in our communities with extravagant church programs and 21st century methodology. While such methods have their place, they can never substitute for personal relationships formed in the context of genuine Christian community.

Don't you think it's time to get back to basics and allow God to build His church through New Testament discipling relationships? It's not too late.

The primary focus of meeting in homes

The primary focus of each house church should be outreach and discipleship, rather than fellowship.Great fellowship will be a healthy by-product of the house church that is consistently reaching out to others.

There will be much prayer and interaction within the group to meet needs and form relationships, but the top priority must always be to bring in the lost. This will cause the house church to mature and reproduce another house church. It will give more believers the opportunity to use the gifts the Lord has given to them to reach the lost and make disciples.

The greatest catalyst for spiritual growth in Christ is turning our eyes from ourselves to Jesus and the needs of those around us. A group of people who are always looking inward, content with the *status quo,* will never grow and multiply. Looking inward prevents growth, like an ingrown toenail, and usually causes pain, competition and stagnation.

When house churches become content to stay the same, without knowing it, they build walls around themselves causing others to feel unwelcome. The group that has a heart to reach out will be willing to change, and will enjoy meaningful fellowship in the process.

When I was newly married and a young missionary, I heard a man of God quote C.T. Studd, the famous missionary: "I do not wish to live 'neath sound of church or chapel bell; I want to run a rescue shop within a yard of hell." These words were life-changing for me.

The main purpose for every house church must be to rescue people from the brink of hell. Otherwise, the house church becomes a social club without any power. The Lord gives us power to be witnesses, not to sit around and enjoy nice comfortable "bless-me" meetings.

> But you will receive power when the Holy Spirit comes on you; and you will be my witnesses in Jerusalem, and in all Judea and Samaria, and to the ends of the earth (Acts 1:8).

The church is not primarily a hospital but an army. Although armies have medical units, the purpose of these units is to get the soldiers well and back on the battlefield in order to destroy the enemy. The focus is not on the medical unit. The focus is on the battle and winning the war.

We are in a spiritual war! We do not have time to sit around and play "church" like children play games. We need to rise up in faith and be the church and destroy the works of darkness in Jesus' name!

When I was a young man, our nation was in the midst of the Vietnam War. Every year, comedian Bob Hope would take an entourage to Vietnam to entertain the soldiers. Now let's face the facts. No one joined the army to see Bob Hope. They went to fight a war. However, while they were there, they had the fringe benefit of being entertained by Bob Hope and his company.

Although the primary purpose of the house church is to reach the lost and disciple new believers, we also experience the fringe benefit of tremendous fellowship and relationships with people who care about us. They stand with us as we face hardships and struggles.

There will be many different creative approaches to reaching the lost and making disciples as we work together in a house church setting; however, the primary vision must be clear and fixed—we are called to fulfill the Great Commission. We don't necessarily fulfill the Great Commission by having an evangelistic teaching at our house

church meetings or going out on the street to eva
week.

When individuals in house churches challenge
beyond themselves to make disciples, they will dis
give them many creative opportunities. Even if no one
to Christ through these opportunities, there is a sp
leased in the house church that keeps our focus on
instead of on ourselves. As we continue to sow, we will eventually
reap.

New churches provide more opportunities for evangelism

Let me remind you again of what Dr. Peter Wagner has told us for years. "The single most effective way to evangelize is to plant new churches."

Fuller Theological Seminary found in a study that if a church is ten or more years old, it takes 85 people to lead one person to Christ. If the church is 4-7 years old, it takes seven people to lead one to Christ. If a church is less than 3 years old, it takes only three people to lead one to Christ (see diagram below): [9]

Age of church	people/salvation ratio
10 years + old	85:1
4-7 years old	7:1
3 years & under	3:1

New churches give the opportunity for more people to come to faith in Christ. Let's plant new churches in homes all over our communities, and reach more people for Jesus! I wholeheartedly ascribe to these words I saw on a plaque at a friend's house: "Save the World, Plant a Church." As house churches are planted, they will rapidly reproduce within an area. The house church network will continue to grow, and there will be more and more opportunities to reach the lost.

A group of new house churches in Keswick, Ontario, is made up of almost all new believers. These new believers bring their friends to the house church meetings. They just love hanging out and talking about life and how the Bible applies to their lives. This generation wants spirituality made real—talk translated into action. House churches provide that place of interaction and authenticity.

churches nurture, develop and release

In addition to multiplying very slowly, current church structures struggle with developing people in their gifts. Canadian Bob Granholm, says:

> Our church buildings are filled with people every Sunday who come and enjoy music and teaching. They experience the joy of fellowship with other believers. Sometimes a non-Christian will even attend, and occasionally that person might be convicted of their sin and be born again. Yet, for the vast majority of people, the Sunday service is an event to enjoy, not a ministry to engage them. Our pews are full of people in whom God has placed good gifts: pastors, teachers, evangelists, prophets and apostles who are not being identified, nurtured and released in their giftings. The current structure does not seem to do this. House churches have the potential to nurture and develop people in areas of gifting, releasing them to be ministers of the gospel as God has gifted and intended. House churches are a runway upon which people can learn by doing, under the mentorship of others.[10]

Some people tell me we do not need any more churches. Let me show you why we need many more churches in our communities. Here is an example. I live in the historically religious community of Lancaster County, Pennsylvania. There are currently about 615 churches in our county. That's a lot of churches! However, when you consider the county's population and the current church attendance at each of these churches, only 17% of the people in our county are involved in the local church.

If 800 new house churches were to be started this year in our county consisting of 25 people each, the church would still only be reaching 21.5% of the population. This puts things in perspective. We need more community churches, more mega-churches and more house churches networking together to reach those without Christ.

In restricted areas, churches can meet in homes

In many cities in America, church buildings are no longer allowed to be built within the city limits because of zoning restrictions. Exploding

urban populations prohibit obtain-
ing real estate to build a church
structure. But believers can meet
in homes! House churches are an
obvious solution to this dilemma.

In some parts of the world,
house churches start as a matter
of necessity born out of other kinds
of legal bans. In the book *House
to House,*[11] I tell the story of a
church in Ethiopia that was forced

**We need community
churches, mega-churches
and house church networks
to work together!**

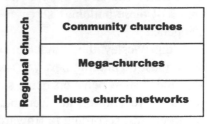

Regional church	Community churches
	Mega-churches
	House church networks

"underground." In 1982, half of all the evangelical churches in Ethiopia
were closed due to harassment, legal banning, and persecution. The
Meserete Kristos Church fell under a complete ban. All of their church
buildings were seized and used for other purposes. Several of their
prominent leaders were imprisoned for years without trial or charges.

The church membership at that time was approximately 5,000. As
the fires of persecution got hotter and hotter each year, they were forced
to go underground and meet in clandestine home groups. Nearly a decade later the Marxist government fell. The same government leaders
who closed the doors of the church buildings a few years earlier, led the
procession of God's people back into the buildings. However, the most
startling news discovered was the church had grown "underground"
from 5,000 to over 50,000 people!

During persecution, these believers met from house to house in
small groups. Hundreds of believers began to get involved in the work
of ministry in these small house churches. They no longer were focusing on the church building or the programs of the church. Their time
together was spent in prayer, reaching the lost, and making disciples.

God's agenda for the building of His kingdom includes two elements—laborers and harvest. He wants laborers trained to bring in the
full harvest: "My food," said Jesus, "is to do the will of him who sent me
and to finish his work. Do you not say, 'Four months more and then the
harvest'? I tell you, open your eyes and look at the fields! They are ripe
for harvest" (John 4:34-36).

Learning from history—the Methodist revival

I have had the privilege of proclaiming the gospel on six continents during the past years. Amazingly, in nearly every nation that I go, I find a Methodist church building! Some of my Methodist friends tell me that many of these buildings serve as memorials to a past revival. What happened?

John Wesley, the founder of the Methodist church, saw that new wine must be put into new wineskins. He started "class meetings" to disciple the new believers being saved during the Methodist revival. A key to the revival was the accountability that the believers found in the small groups, according to Howard A. Snyder, in *The Radical Wesley*:

> The classes were in effect house churches...meeting in various neighborhoods where people lived. The class leaders (men and women) were disciplers.
>
> The classes normally met one evening each week for an hour or so. Each person reported on his or her spiritual progress, or on particular needs or problems, and received the support and prayers of the others . . . According to one author it was, in fact, in the class meeting "where the great majority of conversions occurred."
>
> The class meeting system tied together the widely scattered Methodist people and became the sustainer of the Methodist renewal over many decades. The movement was in fact a whole series of sporadic and often geographically localized revivals which were interconnected and spread by the society and class network, rather than one continuous wave of revival which swept the country. [Classes joined together to form a society.]
>
> Without the class meeting, the scattered fires of revival would have burned out long before the movement was able to make a deep impact on the nation...
>
> Now here is the remarkable thing. One hears today that it is hard to find enough leaders for small groups or for those to carry on the other responsibilities in the church. Wesley put one in ten, perhaps one in five, to work in significant ministry and leadership. And who were these people? Not the educated or the wealthy with time on their hands, but laboring men and

women, husbands and wives and young folks with little or no training, but with spiritual gifts and eagerness to serve...

The system which emerged gave lie to the argument that you can't build a church on poor and uneducated folk. Not only did Wesley reach the masses; he made leaders of thousands of them.[12]

Gradually, however, the Methodist believers put more emphasis on the weekly church meetings in their buildings. As they de-emphasized the accountable relationships they had in their class meetings, the revival movement began to decline. Lord, help us to not make the same mistake in this generation! Let us learn from history that small groups have often served to fan revival throughout church history.

Peter Bunton, in his book, *Cell Groups and House Churches: What History Teaches Us,* mentions that Martin Bucer, a key figure in the Reformation of the church in the 16th century, advocated a radical church reformation to begin in small groups or *Christian communitie*s:

> Indeed he taught that partaking in such little communities modeled on the New Testament was the only way to keep the Ten Commandments.
>
> Additionally, what is of interest is that each group remained connected to others. The leaders were to meet each week, and every one to two months there should be a meeting of all groups in the parish for teaching. (This has some semblance of the structure that Wesley was to establish some two hundred years later!) [13]

Down through history, many movements have emerged to bring the church back to the way it was in the first century. The house church vision is a radical reformation of church structure that fits the New Testament structure of believers meeting in homes. Remember, the early church only started to erect their own buildings more than 250 years after their beginnings.

Once church buildings were erected, believers met in them for the greater part of their church experience. For centuries, the church has become accustomed to Christians gathering in a church building every Sunday, and it is hard to break the mold. However, tradition for traditions' sake gets us in trouble because we begin to trust a method rather than the Living God. Even house church networks become legalistic and traditional if we trust the method or structure rather than allow God to keep us flexible and open to His leading.

Downsizing in order to grow

Downsizing is a familiar term to corporations that face an increasingly stiff competition from competitors in the global economy. Corporations that downsize are trying to rid themselves of unessential costs and liabilities. They may downsize their work force or inventory in order to cut unnecessary costs. This is one way they can continue to exist and expect to be profitable.

Community churches, mega-churches and house churches in a region would do well to work together to utilize all their resources more fully. Why not "downsize" by sharing resources? I believe we will discover myriads of ways that churches, like corporations, can "rid themselves of unessential costs and liabilities."

For example, I look forward to the day when we can be so flexible that we will allow church buildings in our communities to be utilized every day of the week. Many community churches and mega-churches currently use their buildings for a few choice meetings (Sunday morning worship service, midweek prayer meeting, etc.), and the church facility remains unused the rest of the week.

How about this scenario: a community church or mega-church offers (rents?) their facilities to several different house church networks that want to meet in a larger setting each month. The house churches could meet on Sunday nights or on a weeknight when the community or mega-church does not need its facilities. That would be divine efficiency! Money that is saved on constructing new buildings and maintaining old buildings could be given to missions and to the poor.

Sounds pretty simple doesn't it? Is it asking too much for churches to work together like this? Perhaps we have taken the simple gospel and the simplistic New Testament church and complicated it. Let's get back to the simplicity of the gospel and the simplicity of relational church life.

Notes

1. American Society for Church Growth (ASCG), "Enlarging Our Borders," Report presented to the Executive Presbytery, January 1999
2. Ibid.
3. Charles Arn, Institute for American Church Growth, "Enlarging Our Borders," Report presented to the Executive Presbytery, January 1999
4. Ibid.
5. Arden Adamson, secretary-treasurer, Wisconson-Northern Michigan District, "Enlarging Our Borders," Report presented to the Executive Presbytery, January 1999
6. Michael Foust, *Southern Baptist Convention*, "Nine Habits of Effective Evangelistic Churches," June 2001, (quote by Thom Rainer)
7. James H. Rutz, *The Open Church,* (Auburn, Maine: The SeedSowers, 1992), p. 47
8. T. L. Osborne, *Soulwinning Out Where the Sinners Are*, (Tulsa, Oklahoma: Harrison House, 1980). pp. 35,36,37
9. "Enlarging Our Borders," Report presented to the Executive Presbytery, January 1999
10. Bob Granholm, "Proposal for a House Church Network in the Lower Mainland (British Columbia, Canada)," October 1999, www.dawn.ch
11. Larry Kreider, *House to House*, (Ephrata, Pennsylvania: House to House Publications, 1995)
12. Howard A, Synder, *The Radical Wesley*, (Downers Grove, Illinois: Inter-Varsity Press, 1980), pp. 53-57, 63
13. Peter Bunton, *Cell Groups and House Churches: What History Teaches Us,* (Ephrata, PA: House to House Publications, 2001) p. 14

9

Just Keep It Simple

The church in the New Testament was so simple that the common people gladly received the Word of God and met in homes enjoying the Lord's presence and their newfound spiritual family life. They gladly suffered persecution, because Christ had revolutionized their lives.

Years of traditions since those early church days have made the church so complicated. God is calling us back to the simple gospel and the simplistic New Testament church.

Psychologist Larry Crabb, in his book *Connecting,* astutely remarks:

> Maybe the center of Christian community is connecting with a few, where ordinary Christians, whose lives regularly intersect, will accomplish most of the good that we now depend on professionals to provide. That will happen as people connect with each other in ways that only the gospel makes possible.[1]

Sounds pretty simple doesn't it? We need those relational connections in church life. They should be at its very core. In healthy, thriving house churches, people's lives can easily and regularly "intersect."

What should house churches really look like then? How do house church networks operate? I will only be scratching the surface here. Books like Wolfgang Simson's *Houses that Change The World* and Bob Fitt's book *The Church in the House* or a building guide for house churches called *Save The World...Plant a House Church* by Jason Johnston & Rad Zdero can give you more practical insights.[2]

We still have much to learn

Just as we can see and understand only a little about God now, as if we were peering at His reflection in a poor mirror, we have much to learn about how house church networks will work, certainly in our western world. Our vision is a bit hazy and blurred concerning the new way of doing church through house church networks; but within the next few years, I believe we will see more clearly: "The path of the righteous is like the first gleam of dawn, shining ever brighter till the full light of day" (Proverbs 4:18).

Earlier, I mentioned the home school movement that started thirty years ago. In the beginning, only a handful of resources were available to home schoolers. Today, however, there are hundreds of resource centers to assist home school teachers and students. As more house churches are started, I believe we will find increasingly healthy models to which to point as examples.

House churches are real churches

I have spent the past 20 years involved in cell church, and I believe in cell church more than ever. However, we should again make the distinction between a cell church and house church. They are not the same!

First, the cell-based community or mega-churches usually have their own headquarters with an administrative structure. As a cell-based structure, they encourage the real spiritual life to happen in small groups, usually in a home, but it tends to be more meeting-centered with the need for a lot of administration. House churches require no headquarters; they are much more flexible and fluid because they meet solely in homes or other places (coffee shops, offices, etc.) and do not require another building for further church programs.

Second, in the cell-based community or mega-churches, the cell group leaders do not have complete authority as elders of their group in the way that they do in house churches. Instead, cell group leaders are an extension of the leadership of the elders of the local church where believers meet each Sunday in a larger celebration gathering.

House churches are very different because they are self-contained churches in themselves. Each house church has elders (with one of the leaders assuming the primary leadership role of the group) who serve as fathers and mothers with a heart's cry to train and reproduce more leadership within the house church. This kind of fatherly and motherly leader gently nurtures individuals until they are ready to take a step of faith to become leaders themselves.

As we mentioned before, a house church may include several smaller "cell groups" within the house church. These satellite groups often meet at times other than the regular house church meeting time. Smaller groups within the house church often help to foster deeper relationships and greater accountability as people become involved in a lifestyle of everyday community. The house church models a way of life. It takes place entirely outside of the mentality of religious meetings. Church *is* the people living their lives in an extended spiritual family as they focus on reaching the lost. Although families require some organization, it is a relational organization, minus any bureaucracy.

House churches will network

There should be a natural desire for house churches to network with other house churches for encouragement and accountability. If you are living in a rural area and starting a house church, be sure to have a vision to reach out to others and find ways to network together with others in your locale. Most house church networks are regional, but not all. Do not move too fast. The Lord's timing is so important.

Perhaps the Lord will show you where to connect to a house church network that shares your values. Maybe the Lord is calling you to start your own house church network. Some house church networks are small, with only a half dozen or so house churches involved in the network. Others are much larger, with teams of apostolic leaders providing encouragement, oversight, and spiritual protection.

House churches that are not open to becoming a part of a house church network usually become stagnant and focus inward, rather than looking out to the harvest. Although there have been believers involved in house churches for many years throughout America, I do not recommend looking to all of them as a healthy resource.

Not all house churches and house church networks are the same! Although some are healthy, others are unproductive, reactionary and exclusive. Many times, house churches will take on the personality and the value system of the leader. So it is important to know and trust the integrity of the person leading the group and agree with the values, beliefs and practices of the group.

Working together—community churches, mega-churches, house churches

All three kinds of churches working together to form the regional church will have a significant impact in discipling people and changing lives. Some community churches and mega-churches will commission leaders to start house churches and give them the oversight needed to help them grow. Other community churches and mega-churches will "adopt" house churches in their communities and help them network together. Still other community churches will commission future house church leaders to join with house church networks in their region. The fundamental idea is that our Lord's kingdom is being built and expanded in a particular region.

Community churches and mega-churches will interact with house church networks

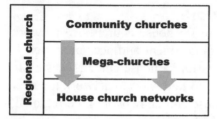

In fact, even though most house churches will continue to birth new house churches, some house churches may actually become community churches. And some of these community churches could become mega-churches. It is all up to the commander-in-chief of the church, our Lord Jesus Christ. There is tremendous freedom in the kingdom of God!

It is possible that some people may be in a house church network for a season, and then be called by God to become involved in a community church or a mega-church. It is the entire regional church that matters. I believe there will be freedom in the coming days in the hearts of God's people to serve wherever God has called them.

"The times, they are a-changing!"

During the industrial age, adults usually kept the same job their entire lives. But in today's information age, studies show that the average person will make at least five career changes during the course of a lifetime. Today's society is a mobile one forcing us to be flexible. This same principle applies in church life.

Each kind of church has its strengths and weaknesses as it endeavors to empower people for ministry. Some new believers may be initially discipled in house churches but eventually become involved in a community church or a mega-church. Therefore, I believe it is important to keep open and friendly relationships with others in church structures that are different from ours. Flexibility is key.

House church networks will interact with community churches and mega-churches

House churches need leadership

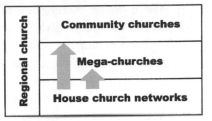

One of the questions I am asked repeatedly is: "Do house churches and house church networks need leadership?" The answer is "yes." Servant leadership. Fatherly leadership. But always some form of godly leadership. If God's appointed leader does not give proper leadership, then the enemy will be sure someone else does who is not God's appointed leadership. The Bible is filled with examples of leadership. Elders were appointed in every church. Teamwork in leadership is so important, but God calls someone to be the primary leader of the team.

In the book *The Cry for Spiritual Fathers and Mothers*[3] I explain how leadership works in the local church in a way that honors the Lord, honors leadership, and honors the people being served. When a house church says they have no need for leadership, the person voicing this the loudest is often the real leader who just does not want to admit it! I am embarrassed by what I have seen in some house churches where they claim there is no leadership, but I am also bothered by what I have seen in some community churches and in some mega-churches where there is autocratic, heavy-handed leadership.

According to Hebrews 13:17, we need to obey and submit to leaders who "keep watch over us." They bring spiritual protection to our lives. We cannot try to blot out this truth from the Bible because unfaithful spiritual leaders have abused it. Obedience and faithfulness to our leaders, however, must always be based on a higher loyalty to God.

I have the privilege of serving as International Director of DCFI, an international apostolic movement. I am blessed to have three spiritual leaders, fathers in the faith, in the greater body of Christ to whom I have submitted myself. Their input into my life brings great security to me and to the leaders with whom I serve.

True apostolic leaders will faithfully serve house churches

All the house churches in the New Testament were submitted to apostolic leaders. Paul tells Titus in Titus 1:5 to appoint elders in every city. These house churches were given apostolic oversight by Titus who served on Paul's apostolic team.

Timing is paramount when it comes to finding an apostolic leader(s) to serve a new house church network. I have friends who lived on the South Island of New Zealand who experienced a move of God in their house church. Within a few months, literally dozens of people came to faith in Christ and became a part of their house church. The leaders of the house church saw the need for proper connection in the body of Christ and for spiritual oversight. Watchman Nee once said, "We do not have authority unless we are under authority."

So, when my friends heard about a new "apostle" who was coming to town, they assumed that they should join with him and the other house churches to which he was giving oversight. However, it did not take long until they found he was a wolf in sheep's clothing, and since he was not under authority, they had no one to turn to.

Within months, this precious work of God in this house church was in shambles because of the abusive "apostle." Paul warns us against false apostles who are not fathers but have a personal agenda. A house church should be sure to take its time in finding true apostolic spiritual oversight.

What about children in house churches?

The Lord values children. They can take an active role in house church life because they are part of the spiritual family in the home. There are many creative options for children.

Many house churches gear the entire meeting to the family and have the children with them the entire time. Here is one mom's experience with children in house church:

> ...all the kids in our group stayed with us. We ate a meal together, took communion together, sang together—the kids often requesting their favorite songs. After singing, one family would do an activity they had prepared that often was a "hands-on" activity or game that offered a godly message or teaching

for the kids. The adults would join the kids in this activity (singles and teens too!). Afterwards, when individuals began to share in the meeting, the kids were given the chance to read any Bible passages that we discussed. Otherwise, the young ones could draw or color while they remained in the room with us, sitting on the couch, snuggled with a parent, sprawled on the living room floor. Of course, much of the discussion went over their heads! They're kids! But they were with us throughout most of our time together, and were permitted to be kids. One of the families had a pool in back and sometimes we'd hold our gathering on their back patio and let the kids swim and have fun together. Now here's the thing: they loved our times of fellowship, and the children all felt like they were extended family with one another—brothers and sisters. They looked forward to any time we got together with any of the other families and had little difficulty communicating with either adults or other kids. When visiting families came, their children were welcomed without reservation.[4]

Children participating in house churches have the privilege of see-ing the Holy Spirit deal and work in real life situations as families meet together as the church. Wolfgang Simson firmly believes that children should be a natural and important part of house churches:

Children are needed to humble us with their questions, break up our endless "adult" discussions, bring us down to earth from our pious clouds, and act as natural evangelists and bridge-builders. They also help us to prove the fruits of the Spirit—patience, for example—and will serve as heaven-sent spies to spot instantly any trace in us of religious superstition and hy-pocrisy." [5]

Another option for children in house churches is for the children to be involved with their parents for about one half of the meeting, and then have someone minister to the children for the rest of the time in another room in the home. Creativity and flexibility are the keys to providing fellowship for kids who want a real walk with God. We have found the book *Biblical Foundations for Children* to be helpful to minister to children in a setting where they have their own special time together (see page 119). I believe that within the next few years, there will be an abundance of resources for children available to house church networks as the Lord defines and refines house churches throughout the world. Let's pray for God's creative solutions and share ideas for children in house churches.

Pitfalls to avoid in house churches
Pride
A common pitfall to avoid in house churches and house church networks is pride. House churches are not the panacea for today's ailing church. If those of us who are called to house church networks take a superior attitude, the Bible tells us we will fall. House church networks are only one of the many things the Lord is doing in the world today. We should never have an exclusive attitude.

Fear
Another trap to avoid is fear. House churches are largely unproven entities in today's church world. They are new for this generation and depend on grassroots leaders to take the initiative. We have to learn to move in faith, and not in fear.

Independent spirit
Still another hidden danger is developing an independent and isolationist spirit. Sometimes those who do not want to come under any type of spiritual authority will gravitate towards house church ministry because they believe they can do their own thing without having to answer to anyone. This kind of independent spirit is a form of pride and will destroy us.

Heresy
House churches may fall into the trap of heresy if they are exclusive and unwilling to work with others. All this can be avoided by being accountable to other leaders in a house church network and the body of Christ at large. We all need accountability to keep us from heresy. The scriptures tell us to receive confirmation from two or three witnesses (2 Corinthians 13:1).

What if I am not called to a house church?

If you are reading this and have no interest whatsoever in becoming involved in a house church network, my admonition to you is to obey the Lord and allow Him to use you in your community church or megachurch. But please guard your heart so you do not persecute the next move of God.

Over the course of history, new moves of God have often persecuted the next wave of God's Spirit. Early reformer Martin Luther persecuted the Anabaptists and had them placed in prison. I have heard some of my Assembly of God pastor friends lament that they persecuted the Charismatic movement of the 1960's and 1970's. This is oddly amazing since both groups believed in the baptism in the Holy Spirit and the manifestation of spiritual gifts. They really should have been in harmony and supporting one another.

Likewise, the cell group movement will need to be careful to guard its heart as the new house church networks spring up alongside the cell group community churches and mega-churches. The church of today is a diverse one, and diversity is healthy. God is working through program-designed churches, cell-based churches, community churches, mega-churches and through house church networks.

So how should those of us called to serve with community churches and mega-churches respond to house church networks that emerge in our community? Let's welcome them, reach out to them and offer them help to succeed. Many of these house church networks may ask to rent our church buildings each month for their monthly celebrations. This would be a win-win situation for both parties!

Let's allow the house church networks to grow up alongside the community churches and the mega-churches in our communities. We need to see ourselves as a part of the regional church the Lord is raising up in these times.

The Charismatic church didn't replace the denominational churches of their day, but grew up right alongside the more traditional churches. Some believers today are leaving Charismatic churches and getting involved in churches that are more traditional. I believe the Lord smiles at us when we get too serious about these things. Those who call on the name of Jesus are everywhere and in every Christian church. Christ has set us free, and we are free indeed (John 8:36)!

What a healthy house church is not

First of all, a healthy house church is not people who are disgruntled with the community or mega-church. Second, a house church is not an ingrown club of people who have forgotten the harvest. Third, it is not Christians who are independent and unwilling to submit to the recognized leaders within the body of Christ because they do not believe in spiritual authority. Fourth, house church networks are not groups of people who have been together for a number of years and have only slightly grown in size or not at all. And finally, healthy house church networks are not groups of people who are stagnant and sterilized by the reasons I have given above.

The churches thrive alongside each other

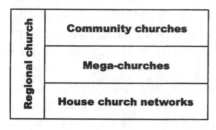

A pastor of a mega-church in our region asked me recently, "How does the house church network fit into the regional church the Lord is restoring in the regions of the world?"

My answer is that it fits like a hand in a glove since it is just another form of church. The only way it will not fit is if the house churches become independent and refuse to work with anyone else. This would be tragic.

Which model of church is most biblical?

You may wonder which of the three models of church is the best or most biblical: the community church, the mega-church, or the house church network? All three! It just depends on which one you are called to. God will use whichever structure He chooses, and He does not necessarily ask for our opinion. A few years ago, I was astounded while sitting with believers in an Anglican church building, Holy Trinity Brompton, in London, England where these believers were experiencing a modern-day move of God. Now the Lord has used them to make the *Alpha Course* available to literally millions of people around the globe.

As soon as we think our group is the only "right" group around town, we get in trouble. Pride always comes before a fall. We must, with great conviction, follow the path the Lord has laid out for us, and at the same time, honor what He is doing through others who are doing it differently than we are.

What the regional church is and is not

Although the purpose of this book is not to expound upon the regional church in detail, a few vital things should be said. There is usually a difference between the local ministerium and the regional church. Local ministers' fellowships, which certainly have their place, often focus on the church business of their community. The regional church has a more far-reaching mandate from the Lord. Its goal is to see Christ proclaimed to every person within the community and to see the entire region transformed by the power of God. The Lord has used George Otis and his *Transformation* videos [6] to open the hearts of pastors and believers all over the world to this truth. The regional church is intended to be a kingdom connection of relationships.

Although it is possible for the local ministerium and the regional church to be one and the same, most often it is not. Why? Because the local ministerium tends to be more bureaucratic while the regional church's intent is to be relational.

While the regional church is represented by the many different denominations within its geographical area, I personally do not believe the regional church will ever replace those denominations. We can benefit from the many flavors of denominational churches within the regional church.

Notes
[1] Larry Crabb, *Connecting*, (Nashville, TN: Word Publishing)
[2] More house church resources:
Wolfgang Simson, *Houses that Change the World,*
(Cumbria, UK: OM Publishing, 1998)
Robert Fitts, *The Church in the House: A Return to Simplicity,*
(order book from: Robert Fitts, 76-6309 Haku Place, Kona, HI 96740)
Jason Johnson & Rad Zdero, *Save the World...Plant a House Church,*
(Ontario, Canada: House Church.Ca, 2000)
[3] *The Cry for Spiritual Fathers & Mothers,* Larry Kreider, (Ephrata, PA: House to House Publications, 2000), pp. 151-160
[4] Homechurch.org, posted 05-18-2001, by Lisa C. from Florida
[5] Wolfgang Simson, *Houses that Change the World,* (Cumbria, UK: OM Publishing, 1998), p. 96
[6] *Transformations (Documentary Video)*, Otis, George Jr, host, Publisher: The Sentinel Group

10
The Time is Now!

If you build it, they will come!

You may remember the popular movie *Field of Dreams*. A farmer hears an "inner" voice and builds a baseball diamond in his cornfield, out in the middle of nowhere. Baseball legends mysteriously appear, and the fans flock there from miles around.

In the real world, in biblical history, God instructed His people to build by following a pattern. If they followed the pattern, He promised to come! In Exodus 25:8-9, God gives His instruction for building the tabernacle. The tabernacle was to be a sanctuary or a place set apart for the Lord to dwell among His people: "Then have them make a sanctuary for me, and I will dwell among them. Make this tabernacle and all its furnishings exactly like the pattern I will show you." If we follow God's pattern, He will come, and in the process, release new kinds of structures or wineskins for the church. To be successful, the infrastructure of the church must be built after God's pattern.

According to God's sovereign wisdom, He has a time and season for His plans. Again and again in scripture, we notice how God's people are often unaware of what He is doing or wants to do. When God sent the Messiah, many of God's people were blind to what Jesus' purpose was on this earth. Today, the church often does not discern when God is fulfilling His purposes on earth.

In 1 Chronicles 12:32, the men of Issachar are mentioned because they had an understanding of the times and discerned what God was about to do (bring David to the throne): "Men of Issachar, who understood the times and knew what Israel should do—200 chiefs, with all their relatives under their command."

The leaders of Issachar not only knew what Israel should do, they agreed how to do it. In addition, the leaders were in unity with the 200 "relatives under their command." This group was not a large group, but their unity and oneness of purpose was invaluable in fulfilling God's purposes during this critical time in history.

The time is now to hear God's voice and join Him to fulfill His purposes here on earth. Rick Joyner, a prophetic voice in today's church, recently wrote in his *Prophetic Bulletin* that he believes a major awakening will soon occur within the church, and discerning leaders will be ready for it:

> A revolution is coming to Christianity that will eclipse the Reformation in the sweeping changes that it brings to the church. When it comes, the present structure and organization of the church will cease to exist, and the way that the world defines Christianity will be radically changed.
>
> What is coming will not be a change of doctrine, but a change in basic church life. The changes that are coming will be so profound that it will be hard to relate the present form of church structure and government to what is coming. The new dynamic of church life will overshadow the Great Awakenings in their social impact, transforming cities and even whole nations. It will bring a sweeping sense of righteousness and justice to the whole earth.
>
> The future leaders of the church are now being given a vision of radical New Testament Christianity being restored to the earth. It is time to heed the call and allow the Lord to lead His people to the new wineskins that will be able to hold what is about to break out upon the earth. Whenever there is a choice to make between the new and the old, choose the new. To be a part of what is coming, we must have the faith of Abraham who was willing to leave the security of the known to seek God in unknown places. The future leaders of the church will be willing to risk all to seek the city that God is building, not man.[1]

A new model for a new time

I, too, believe we must "allow the Lord to lead His people to the new wineskins that will be able to hold what is about to break out upon the earth." Today, I have the same sense of expectancy about the new house church networks that I had about cell churches emerging more than twenty years ago. Many future pastors are sitting on church pews today, finding no room for their gifts to be released in their present structures. We must allow a radical kind of Christianity that becomes a life force to break out and motivate our future leaders to action. House church networks enable the priesthood of all believers, and require no expensive church buildings. Every believer will begin to realize his or her part to play in discipling the nations. As a result, house churches meeting in every community will cover our nation within the next few years.

My friends, Steve and Mary Prokopchak, from Elizabethtown, Pennsylvania, led a cell group that ballooned to 85 people a few years ago. The small group kept growing and growing because no one in their cell group thought they could lead like Steve and Mary. The Prokopchaks soon realized they needed to spend more time in developing and encouraging future leaders within their group so they could multiply the cell group.

They approached the problem by breaking into five small prayer groups within the cell group, and appointing one leader for each prayer group. As cell leaders, Steve and Mary could then easily mentor the prayer group leaders. Eventually, the leaders felt confident enough to lead on their own and started to meet in separate homes. Four new cell groups were started in a relatively short time, because people were encouraged to take that step of faith.

Multiplying people is not that hard to do. A group should continually speak the vision of growth and multiplication and the fact that healthy families have the expectation that their children will eventually grow up and start their own families. A good leader will focus his or her time and energy in training faithful, potential leaders. Most potential leaders do not think they have what it takes to be leaders. They need to be encouraged.

One time, in our church, we invited more than two dozen potential cell leaders to a restaurant, prayed for them individually and encouraged the potential we saw in their lives to lead. One year later, nearly all of them were serving in leadership in cell ministry.

Why are many future spiritual leaders seated in church pews every Sunday or even attending a small group unaware that they could be leading a church? They are inactive because the only models they have ever seen are the community church model and the mega-church model. As we have seen in this book, these are not the only models available.

The house church network gives us a new model. It puts everyone on a more even playing field. I believe there are thousands of future house church pastors who will have faith to lead 20-40 believers in a house church as a spiritual father or mother, but they would never want to lead 100+ people and attempt to maintain the many programs and ministries, in addition to a building project, that a traditional church structure often requires.

We need many more churches

We do not need fewer churches in our communities: we need more! The house church model gives many more believers the opportunity to start new churches. I believe there are thousands of former pastors and Christian leaders who are no longer involved in church leadership because they have retired or are now working in the marketplace, unaware that they could be starting a brand new church in their home, giving opportunity for more people to be exposed to the gospel. Many unsaved people in our communities will not enter a church building, but they will come into our homes. Churches in homes, led by humble spiritual moms and dads, are not only a wave of the future; they are the need of the future!

House churches will be diverse

House churches and house church networks will not all look the same. I believe there will be many variations and hybrids. With all the new models, it will be hard to keep up as the Lord's people follow His Spirit. Since house churches are decentralized, they do not require lots of organization and administration. To keep administration to a minimum, some house church networks will share an office in their city. Why have 20 copiers when you only need one? In some house church networks, the leadership of the house churches will give a tithe of the money they receive in their house church to the overseers of the house church network in their area. In other house church networks, the leaders will give their personal tithe to those over them in the Lord. Others will do both. Still others will have a looser connection with the leadership of the house church network.

Young leaders with a vision

I am currently working with a group of young leaders who are starting a house church network in my home area of Lancaster County, Pennsylvania. It is still in its infant stages, but it has begun. I am going to help them in any way that I can and try to stay out of the way!

One of the young house church planters took a group of us into the basement in his home. He showed how he is dry-walling his basement in preparation for the new house church he plans to start in the near future. He is planning to mount a video projector on his basement ceiling and use PowerPoint technology to project words to worship songs against the wall of his basement. He told us he could also use this for teaching videos to train believers in his home. I was amazed. I had never thought about anything like this.

I have another young friend (not involved with the Lancaster group) who wants to open up his coffee shop for a house church to reach out to those in his city.

The leaders of the Lancaster group have designed a vision for the new house church network they are starting. It states:

> The vision for this house church network is to create new, flexible wineskins that will be a leadership training ground for rapid reproduction of leaders of small, relational, evangelistic churches. These new churches could meet in homes, campuses, places of business, malls, coffee shops, barns, skate parks, and other places where people naturally meet.
>
> Spiritual parents will be trained to mentor new believers, new small group leaders, new church leaders and new apostolic leaders. The leadership of each church would have the freedom and authority to give the church the flavor they sense the Lord directing them to have, within biblical guidelines. These new churches could meet on any day or night of the week and would network together by the direction of the Holy Spirit.

Working together

DOVE Christian Fellowship International, the worldwide network of cell-based churches that I and a team of spiritual leaders oversee, is broadening our territory to include house church networks. We realize that cell-based community churches, cell-based mega-churches and house church networks, although different, are close cousins. Our experience thus far has been mostly with cells in a mega-church and with cells in community churches.

In light of this, we are adding special training to our current leadership training school for house church planters. Brian Sauder, director of the school, aims to "emphasize that there can be cells in house churches, cells in community churches and cells in mega-churches. If we want all three types of churches to coexist, we will need to be proactive in training for all three."

All the churches are part of the Lord's plan for every region

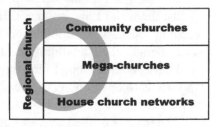

We want to stay current with what the Lord is doing in our day and work with the existing churches as well. We believe we are called by the Lord to help start new cell-based community churches, cell-based mega-churches, and cell-based house churches that form house church networks, because all three types of churches are a part of the Lord's plan for His church in every region. Leaders of all denominations and movements will also be wise to reach out to those within their family of churches and help them start house church networks, otherwise future house church leaders within their denominations will look elsewhere for spiritual oversight.

The fivefold minister's role in house churches

One of the secrets to John Wesley's Methodist house churches and exponential kingdom growth were the circuit riders. These fivefold ministers were the spiritual specialists who traveled from house church to house church. God is raising modern-day fivefold ministers in His church today: "It was he who gave some to be apostles, some to be prophets, some to be evangelists, and some to be pastors and teachers, to prepare

God's people for works of service, so that the body of Christ may be built up" (Ephesians 4:11-12).

Fivefold apostles, prophets, evangelists, pastors and teachers are ministers who circulate within the house churches to train and equip leaders. Their goal is to strategically release people into their God-given calling, according to Wolfgang Simson, thus providing a large leadership structure to grow within the house churches:

> [The fivefold ministers] function as a spiritual blood-circulation system by nurturing all house churches with the elements necessary to become or remain healthy and therefore to multiply. Those ministries are like sinews and joints, linking the various house churches together to be a whole system. Their ministry transcends the individual house church and serves the body of Christ like a spiritual gene pool, which the house churches of an area or a region, and sometimes beyond, can draw from.[2]

Fivefold ministers are spiritual fathers and mothers called to train the next generation in their specific gifts and calling. They speak with the Lord's authority because they represent one of the ministry gifts of Jesus Christ. The Lord sent these fivefold parents to us that we might be complete, lacking nothing. The Lord validates them by the evidence of spiritual fruit, changed lives and signs following their ministry such as miracles. They are recognized by local church leadership because they have been raised themselves in the trenches and released into ministry. How does it happen? How are the fivefold ministers grown in the first place?

As an individual serves and allows God to shape his character in his house church, his gifts and anointings will become apparent. He is then recognized and given greater responsibility. Experienced fivefold fathers will recognize his gift and mentor him. Apostolic fathers will train younger apostolic ministers, prophetic fathers train younger prophets in prophetic ministry and so on, so that the body of Christ is equipped, encouraged and comes to maturity.

Our view is that many of these "fivefold" ministry gifts are for trans-local ministry, not to be used solely in one cell group, house church, or congregation as seen in Acts 15:22, 30-32, 35. These gifts should be far-reaching as they minister to every level of the church: individuals, families, cell groups, house churches, community churches, mega-churches, movements, and the church at large.

Apostles, prophets, evangelists, pastors, teachers help the church come to maturity

Apostles are given to the church to help us receive a vision from the Lord to reach the world. Prophets are given to train us to listen to the voice of God. Evangelists are called of God to stir and train us to reach the lost. Pastors are commissioned by the Lord to encourage and show us how to make disciples! And teachers have a divine anointing to assist us in understanding the Word of God. Most fivefold ministers also have a "gift mix." For example, someone may be a prophetic teacher or a teaching evangelist. The apostle, prophet, evangelist, pastor and teacher must learn how to function together in order for the church of Jesus Christ to come to a place of maturity.

The church, which is going to grow, is the church that makes sure they are receiving a regular impartation from each of these ministry gifts while realizing that only Jesus has all of the gifts. House churches give an excellent opportunity to receive from each of these trans-local ministry gifts. This is why it is important for people with the various gifts to minister the Word in the house churches. We need to hear from each of the five ministry gifts. If your house church is lacking a zeal for evangelism, ask an evangelist to come and minister to you for a few weeks. Then see if any of the believers in your house church are willing to go with him to share his faith with an unsaved person. You will be amazed at the results!

The house church network will open the door for hundreds and thousands of fivefold ministers to minister to God's people according to their own gifts and calling. There are only so many mega-churches and community churches to go around, and many community church and mega-church pastors prefer to do much of the preaching and teaching each Sunday. But house church leaders think differently. They are looking for specialists in the body of Christ who can come into their house church and minister according to the gift that the Lord has given to the fivefold minister. Since there will not be as much overhead with building mortgages and maintenance in the house church, they can give monetary gifts and love offerings to support these fivefold ministry specialists.

House church networks and missions

Traditionally, western missionaries have had a tendency to export the only type of wineskin they have experienced—the community church or the mega-church. Missionaries who are sent out of house church networks already have experienced basic Christian community and New Testament church life from house to house. They will not need to un-learn much of what they may have experienced in order to effectively minister the gospel in unreached areas of the world. Since house church networks follow the simple pattern in the book of Acts, they can work in any nation or culture.

Release flexible containers!

Floyd McClung pastors Metro Christian Fellowship in Kansas City. He asked me to speak at his church and help train a few hundred small group leaders on a Saturday morning before the multiple weekend ser-vices. Floyd made a statement to his small group leaders that I will never forget: "There are young leaders among us who will be planting new churches from our church. Many may be house churches, and some of them may not even be a part of our church. Maybe they will join up with another movement, but either way, we must get behind them and help them." We must take this posture as the Lord prompts the next generation to plant new house churches and house church networks right in our own back yards. These house churches are needed to contain, nurture, and equip the harvest that is ready to be reaped in our communities and in the nations.

My friend Mike Bickle, director of International House of Prayer of Kansas City, has often shared that God had revealed to him that "God is going to change the forms and expressions of church within one generation to a great degree." Recently he expressed that "the house church network is a vital ingredient in that change."

In 2 Kings 4:1-7 the story is told of Elisha miraculously multiplying the oil of a poor widow. As long as the widow had vessels to pour the oil into, the flow of oil continued. But when she ran out of vessels, the supply of new oil was halted. In many ways, this story is a prophetic picture of the present purpose of God for the church. He has promised to pour out His Holy Spirit in these last days, but this will necessitate flexible containers to hold the great harvest that is on the horizon. Is it possible that the Lord is waiting for His church to prepare the proper containers so He can fully pour out His Spirit?

Now is the time to prepare leaders for the coming harvest. We cannot force new Christians into our old wineskins—we must prepare new wineskins for the new wine. Forming new vessels will facilitate the Lord's commission to make disciples. Many new types of vessels, including new house churches networking together in our communities, must be formed. Let's get "about our Father's business."

To be continued...as these new house church networks continue to emerge across the nations!

Notes
[1] Rick Joyner, *The Morning Star Prophetic Bulletin*, "Revolution," May 2000
[2] Wolfgang Simson, *Houses that Change the World,* (Cumbria, UK: OM Publishing, 2001), p. 123

APPENDIX ONE

Questions Most Often Asked

About House Church Networks
and the Regional Church

What is the difference between a community church, a mega-church and a house church network?

A community church (a church of approximately 50-1,000) and mega-church (generally a church of over 1,000) function within traditional church structure. They meet in church buildings every Sunday morning and may or may not have cell groups meeting in homes during the week. The community church reaches out to its local community and compares to a neighborhood store, which has a similar scope of influence. The mega-church, however, could be compared to the Wal-Mart superstore because it reaches a wider area. People in mega-churches often travel longer distances to attend meetings, which offer a broad range of services.

The house church networks are entirely different from the community and mega-churches because each house church is a church in itself with its own elders and leadership. These house church networks are like the average stores in a shopping mall because each church needs to network with others in order to flourish. They meet as a church in homes or other locations that do not require constructing buildings to accommodate a larger group. They focus on growing by starting new house churches. (See Chapters Three and Four: pages 17-38)

What is the difference between a house church and a cell church?

House churches are self-contained churches in themselves; they are not just home groups within a wider church structure. A large gap separates the two. The cell-based community churches or mega-churches usually have their own headquarters with an administrative structure. House churches require no headquarters; they are much more flexible and fluid because they meet solely in homes or other places (coffee shops, offices, etc.) and do not require another building for further church programs.

In cell-based community churches and mega-churches, the cell group leaders are an extension of the leadership of the elders of the local church where believers meet each Sunday in a larger celebration gathering. House churches are entire churches by themselves. Each house church has elders who serve as fathers and mothers with a heart's cry to train and reproduce more leadership within the house church. House churches also may have a few small satellite cells to help disciple new believers and give hands-on training for future house church leaders.

The house church models a way of life. It takes place entirely outside of the mentality of religious meetings. Church becomes people living their lives in an extended spiritual family as they focus on reaching the lost. Although families require some organization, it is a relational organization, minus the bureaucracy. (See pages 9-12, 82-83)

What if a house church is not a part of a house church network?
The reason for house church networks is to provide accountability and encouragement to individual house churches. Exclusiveness is unhealthy for a house church. Every house church really should be connected to others in some way. (See pages 15-16, 83)

Could some community churches or mega-churches adopt house churches?
All three kinds of churches can help to disciple people and change lives. Some community churches and mega-churches will commission leaders to start house churches. Some community church and mega-church leaders will give them the oversight needed to help them grow. Other community churches and mega-churches will "adopt" house churches in their communities and help them network together. (See page 84)

Could some house churches become community churches or mega-churches?
Even though most house churches will continue to birth new house

churches, some house churches may actually become community churches. And some of these community churches could become mega-churches. There is tremendous freedom in the kingdom of God! (See page 84)

Which of these three kinds of churches is best or most biblical?

All three! It just depends on which one you are called to. God will use whichever structure He chooses, and He does not necessarily ask us for our opinion. As soon as we think our group is the only "right" group around town, we get in trouble. Pride always comes before a fall. We must, with great conviction, follow the path the Lord has laid out for us, but honor what He is doing through others who are doing it differently than we are. (See pages 90-91)

Do we need leadership in house churches and house church networks?

Yes. Servant leadership; fatherly leadership, but always some form of godly leadership. If God's appointed leader does not give proper leadership, then the enemy will be sure someone else does who is not God's appointed leadership. The Bible is filled with examples of team leadership and leadership among the team. (See page 85)

Will every young person get involved in a house church network?

No, many will be called by the Lord to serve in community churches while others serve in mega-churches. But many young people today will get involved in house church networks because it fits the value system of their generation. (See page 3-4, 89)

What about children in house churches?

The Lord values children. They can take an active role in house church life because they are part of the spiritual family. There are many creative options for children. Many house churches gear the entire meeting to the family and have the children with them the entire time.

Other house churches, like many cell groups, have the children involved with their parents for about one half of the meeting, and someone in the house church ministers to the children for the rest of the time in another room. (See pages 86-87)

What are some pitfalls and traps to avoid in house church networks?

A common pitfall and trap to avoid in house churches and house church networks is pride. House churches are not the panacea for today's ailing church. If those of us who are called to house church networks take a superior attitude, the Bible tells us we will fall. Another pitfall to avoid is fear. We have to learn to move in faith, and not in fear. A further pitfall is developing an independent and isolationist spirit. House churches may also fall into the pitfall of heresy if they are exclusive and unwilling to work with others. (See page 88)

How should those of us called to serve with community churches and mega-churches respond to house church networks that emerge in our community?

Let's welcome them, reach out to them and offer to help them succeed. We must allow the house church network to grow up along side the community churches and the mega-churches in our communities and realize we are all a part of the regional church the Lord is raising up. (See pages 35-38, 84, 89)

Could you tell me what a house church network is not?

First of all, a house church is not people who are disgruntled with the community or mega-church. Second, a house church is not an ingrown club of people who have forgotten the harvest. Third, it is not Christians who are independent and unwilling to submit to the recognized leaders within the body of Christ because they do not believe in spiritual authority. Fourth, house church networks are not groups of people who have been together for a number of years and have only slightly grown in size or not at all. (See page 90)

How does the house church network fit into the regional church the Lord is restoring in geographical regions of the world?

More and more leaders from all kinds of churches are realizing the need for healthy relationships to be established between churches in a community. The house church network fits the regional church like a hand in a glove since it is just another form of church. The only way it will not fit is if the house churches become independent and refuse to work with anyone else or if the existing churches do not accept house churches. (See pages 35-38, 91)

What is the difference between the local ministerium and the regional church?

There is a big difference between the local ministerium and the regional church. Local ministers' fellowships (local ministeriums) usually focus on the church business of their community. The regional church focuses on prayer and relationships and has a mandate from the Lord to see Christ proclaimed to every person within his or her community and the region transformed by the power of God. (See page 91)

Will the regional church replace denominations?

The regional church is *not* an attempt to do away with denominations and get back to separating believers on the basis of geographical distance exclusively. I believe we have to work with what we have today. This means that the local churches within a collective regional church will probably each maintain their denominational flavor, while working in a unified manner to more effectively share Christ in their geographical area. I personally do not believe the regional church will ever replace denominations, because we need many flavors of church in our communities. (See page 36, 91)

How are leaders chosen for the regional church?

There are many ways for like-minded leaders to unify and take on the challenge to reach their regions for Christ. I am excited about a local regional Christian leadership group that has recently emerged in our region. This regional leadership group is not an organization to join, but a network of leaders devoted to relationships. Through prayer and fasting, the leadership community has appointed 26 leaders to work together on a leadership council to oversee the leadership community. Council members include Christian leaders from many types of churches, leaders in business, key ministry leaders and even a County Commissioner. Some are members of community churches, others members of mega-churches, while others are members of a new house church network. The regional council has prayerfully chosen seven from among them to consider leading the council as an executive team. Presently, four of the seven have begun to serve while the other three are waiting for the Lord's timing to serve on the team. We asked one of the leaders of the four to serve as a team leader, and he is currently taking that responsibility. (See pages 36-38)

What is DOVE Christian Fellowship International?

DOVE Christian Fellowship International (DCFI) started with a group of young Christian believers who had a burden to reach out in love to the unchurched youth in their local community in northern Lancaster County, Pennsylvania.

It was the early 1970's and the time of a nationwide awakening among young people in the United States. The nation had been through tumultuous times in the 1960's with rapid changes tearing at the fabric of our society, including the sexual revolution, Vietnam War, women's liberation and abortion rights.

The church was challenged to be a force in those uncertain times. After a decade of young people dabbling in the occult and drug culture seeking answers for life but being disillusioned, they were now turning to God in great numbers.

Christian song writers and screenwriters producing songs like, "I Wish We'd All Been Ready," and a movie entitled, "A Thief In The Night," describing possible end-time scenarios, jolted Christian young people from their complacency. Many of these young people developed a genuine burden for their world, because the end seemed near.

It was in these times that a group of us, who were Christian young people living in south-central Pennsylvania, started an organization called "The Lost But Found." Through friendship evangelism, we saw many young people come to know Jesus as their Lord. A Bible study under the direction of Larry Kreider called "Rhema Youth Ministries" nurtured many of these young Christians.

New wineskins for the new wine

Although we had tried to get the new believers to whom we were relating involved, they simply didn't fit into the established churches in our community. It seemed clear there was a need for new church structures flexible enough to relate to new converts from a variety of backgrounds. That's why Jesus said we need to put new wine into new wineskins: "Nor do they put new wine into old wineskins, or else the wineskins break, the wine is spilled, and the wineskins are ruined. But they put new wine into new wineskins, and both are preserved" (Matthew 9:16-17).

Increasingly, there became a need for a flexible New Testament-style church (new wineskin) that could relate to and assist these new believers (new wine) in their spiritual growth. In 1978, God spoke to Larry about being "willing to be involved with the underground church."

Our adventure into cell groups

So began our church's adventure into cell groups. A cell group was started in Larry and LaVerne Kreider's home and when their living room was filled to capacity, they turned over the responsibility to leaders they had trained and started a second cell in another home. The roots began to grow for an "underground church" where believers were nourished in these "underground" cell groups as they gathered to pray, evangelize and build relationships with each other. We believed when the underground roots (individuals in relationship in cell groups) are healthy, the whole church is strong.

By the time our church, DOVE Christian Fellowship, officially began in October, 1980, there were approximately 25 of us meeting in a large living room on Sunday mornings and in three cell groups during the week. We discovered cell groups to be places where people have the opportunity to experience and demonstrate Christianity built on relationships, not simply on meetings. In the cell groups, people could readily share their lives with each other and reach out with the healing love of Jesus to a broken world. We desired to follow the pattern in the New Testament church as modeled in the book of Acts, as the believers met from house to house.

Twelve years later, as these cell groups continued to grow and to multiply, more than 2,300 believers were meeting in over 125 cell groups all over south-central Pennsylvania. Churches were planted in Scotland, Brazil, Kenya, and New Zealand. Believers met in cell groups in homes during the week and in clusters of cells in geographical areas for celebration meetings each Sunday morning. Here believers received teaching, worshipped together and celebrated what the Lord was doing during the week through the cell groups. Every few months the entire church would meet together to worship on a Sunday morning in a large gymnasium or in a local park.

Several times, we closed down our Sunday celebration meetings for a four-week period and met in home cell groups on Sunday mornings to strengthen the vision for building the church underground. During one of those times, we came back together after a month of meeting solely in cell groups and realized the Lord had added 100 people to the church.

We made our share of mistakes

Although the church had grown rapidly in a relatively short span, we made our share of mistakes. The Lord began to deal with pride and unhealthy control in our lives. We found the Lord's purpose for cell groups was to release and empower His people, not to control them. We repented before the Lord and before His church.

Our cell-based church had reached a crossroads. We were experiencing the pain of gridlock among some of our leadership. There was an exodus of some good leaders from our ranks. It was painful, and Larry Kreider, who was serving as the senior pastor, almost quit.

In retrospect, we feel the mistakes we made were partly due to our immaturity as leaders and partly due to not having an outside accountability team to help us when we ran into conflicts in decision-making. Perhaps the Lord in His providence was repositioning some of His players elsewhere in the body of Christ.

But the Lord kept taking us back to the original vision He had given, calling us to be involved with the "underground church." Today we walk with a spiritual limp, but we are so grateful to the Lord for what He taught us during those days.

Transition

It became clear that in order for DOVE (an acronym for "Declaring Our Victory Emmanuel") to accomplish what we were originally called to accomplish, we needed to adjust our church government and "give the church away." The vision the Lord had given us, "to build a relationship with Jesus, with one another, and reach the world from house to house, city to city and nation to nation," could not be fulfilled under our current church structure. We recognized the Lord had called us to be an apostolic movement, but we did not know how it should be structured.

It took more than two years to prepare for this transition. On January 1, 1996, our church in the USA became eight individual churches, each with their own eldership team. We formed an Apostolic Council to give spiritual oversight to DCFI, and Larry Kreider was asked to serve as its International Director. The Apostolic Council gave each church eldership team the option of becoming a part of the DCFI family of churches and ministries or connecting to another part of the body of Christ. Each of these eight churches expressed a desire to work together to plant churches throughout the world and became a part of the DCFI family. The majority of the overseas church plants also desired to become a part of the DCFI family of churches and ministries.

We have found apostolic ministry provides a safe environment for each congregation and ministry partnering with DCFI to grow and reproduce themselves. This new model emphasizes leading by relationship and influence rather than hands-on-management. A senior elder and team (we prefer to call the leader of a congregation a *senior elder*, rather than senior pastor, simply because he may or may not have the actual gift of a pastor) have a leadership gift to equip believers to do the work of ministry in cell groups within a congregation. The Apostolic Council members are responsible to spend time in prayer and the ministry of the Word and give training, oversight and mentoring to local church leadership. They also are called to give clear vision and direction to the entire movement.

Becoming an apostolic movement

Unlike an "association of churches," which gives ordination and general accountability to church leaders, we see an "apostolic movement" as a family of churches with a common focus—a mandate from God to labor together to plant and establish churches throughout the world. Although some may call us a new denomination, we prefer the terminology "apostolic movement." We do not mind being called a new denomination, but denominationalism often separates us rather than focuses on our need for the Lord and for each other. We believe each denomination and movement has a redemptive purpose from God, and we need to honor, serve and learn from each other. We build on the shoulders of those who have gone on before us.

As a cell-based church planting movement, we are intent on training a new generation of church planters and leaders just waiting for a chance to spread their wings and fly! We are called to mobilize and empower God's people (individuals, families, cells and congregations) at the grassroots level to fulfill His purposes. Every cell group should have a vision to plant new cells. Every church should have a God-given vision to plant new churches.

Partnering together

For many years, we knew we were called to plant new churches, but a few years ago, the Lord spoke to Larry, "I have many orphans in my body, and I am calling you to adopt some of my orphans." We knew He was calling us to also open our hearts to cell-based churches who had no spiritual oversight and apostolic protection. Now, in addition to church planting and multiplication, the Lord has given us a process of adopting churches who are called to partner with us. After going through a one-year engagement process of discernment, churches with similar values and vision are becoming partner churches with the DCFI family. Ron Myer works with a team of leaders who give oversight to this engagement process in the USA, as others do on other continents.

Our transition from one church into several churches has allowed the old structure to die so we could experience the new—a network of cell-based churches partnering together. This network of churches started just over five years ago. At the time of this writing, there are currently over 80 cell-based congregations either in the engagement period or partnering with the DCFI family from nations in four continents of the world. There are churches in the United States, Kenya, Uganda, New Zealand, Scotland, Croatia, Bulgaria, Canada, and Barbados. The Lord has taken us on an amazing ride during the past few years.

Our desire is to see congregations of cell groups clustered together in the same area so leaders can easily meet as regional presbyteries for prayer and mutual encouragement, and to find ways to be more effective in building His kingdom together. Senior elders of DOVE churches in Pennsylvania have the blessing of meeting together each month for prayer and mutual encouragement. This same pattern is encouraged in other regions where DCFI partner churches are in close proximity to one another. An Apostolic Council member also meets regularly and individually with each senior elder.

Each DCFI partner church is governed by a team of elders and consists of believers committed to one another in cell groups. Each cell and each local church has its own identity while being interdependent with the rest of the DCFI family.

Networking with the body of Christ

We believe another important aspect to kingdom building is networking with other churches and ministries outside of the DCFI family. In this way, we can resource one other. There is no single church or family of churches who has it all! We welcome the exchange of Christian leaders between the DCFI apostolic movement and others in the body of Christ as we learn from the rest of God's family and share what the Lord has given to us. DCFI partner church leaders are encouraged to pray regularly with other pastors in their region. DOVE leaders are all encouraged to participate in pastors' gatherings in their region.

God has given us a wonderful support team at DCFI consisting of the Apostolic Council, a team of Fivefold Translocal Ministers, a Stewardship Council which handles the administration of financial details and legalities, and various ministries who are committed to resource the leadership and believers in DCFI partner churches and serve the greater body of Christ.

These various ministries offer leadership training and ministry development on many levels. An essential twenty-four-hour Prayer Ministry includes a team of "prayer generals" who recruit, train and encourage a team of "prayer warriors" responsible to cover segments of time each week while praying for the entire DCFI family twenty-four hours a day. Nelson Martin oversees this vital prayer ministry.

The International Apostolic Council and leadership from DCFI partner churches throughout the world meet together each March for our annual DCFI International Leadership Conference at a conference center on the east coast of the USA for the purpose of mutual encouragement, leadership training, relationship building, and to receive a common vision from the Lord. DCFI partner church leaders also gather each year regionally and/or nationally for strategic prayer, relationship building, leadership training and mutual encouragement. We believe the Lord has called us to work as a team together—*with a shared vision, shared values, a shared procedure, and to build together by relationship.*

In order for the DCFI family of churches and ministries to be effective in laboring together, we wrote our procedure, including constitution and by-laws, in a handbook. This *DCFI Leadership Handbook* is available by contacting the DCFI Office at 717-738-3751.

Training and releasing God's people

An important philosophy of ministry at DCFI is to release each believer and local leadership in order to provide a delegation of authority and responsibility to all believers. Unless elders can release responsibility and authority to the cell leaders at a cell group level, this principle will not work. In this way, the Lord releases every believer to be a minister.

Every church leader is encouraged to maintain his security in the Lord and take the risk of empowering and releasing cell leaders to minister to others by performing water baptisms, serving communion, praying for the sick, giving premarital counseling, and discipling new believers. A major aspect of cell ministry is preparing and training future spiritual fathers and mothers. And many of these cell leaders will be future elders and church planters. They are experiencing "on the job training."

Brian Sauder gives oversight to the *House to House Church Planting and Leadership School.* This leadership training school is now being used to train cell leaders, pastors and elders in cell-based community churches, mega-churches and house churches throughout the body of Christ. It is both a live school and a video correspondence school used as a satellite school in churches throughout the world.

The philosophy here is to train them to give them away! We expect the believers in our cell groups and churches will soon have their own families—new cell groups and new churches that they plant.

Fivefold translocal ministry

According to Ephesians 4:11-12, the five ministry gifts of the apostle, prophet, evangelist, pastor and teacher are called by the Lord to equip the saints to minister and encourage the body of Christ. Within the DCFI family, fivefold ministers who have proven ministries and are recommended by their elders as having a larger sphere of ministry than their own cell and local church, are recognized and affirmed by the Apostolic Council to serve translocally. These translocal ministers are often invited by other cell groups and local churches for ministry.

DCFI missions outreaches

During the past two decades, DOVE has sent hundreds of short and long term missionaries to the nations. Each long-term missionary is "embraced" by a cell group, a local church, and by individuals from DCFI partner churches. A team of people joins a missionary's support team by giving financially and praying for the missionary. Cells who "embrace" a missionary or missionary family pray for them, write to them, and serve the missionary practically while on furlough or during times of crisis.

Bruce Heckman, who oversees DOVE Mission International, and his team endeavor to serve all DOVE missionaries who are sent out from DCFI partner churches regardless of which "field" they serve on. Some missionaries are directly involved in the DCFI church planting "field," while others may serve instead with the YWAM "field" or with some other missions agency. We are called to build the kingdom, not just our own network of churches. Yet, as a network of churches, we are called by the Lord as a family to plant new cell-based churches together in the unreached areas of the world.

Our long-term goal is to establish many apostolic councils in various regions of the world. There are currently six regional apostolic leadership teams consisting of apostolic leaders who are responsible for oversight of DCFI churches in six regions of the world. Eventually, we believe the leadership for the DCFI movement will be a true DCFI International Apostolic Council, whose members will include apostolic leaders from many nations. This International Apostolic Council will be responsible for the spiritual oversight and mentoring of apostolic leaders and apostolic councils located around the world.

The vision continues

The Bible tells us that without a vision the people perish. The DCFI family is called to keep actively involved in what the Lord is doing in the world and participate in the present expressions of His anointing. We desire to empower, train, and release God's people at the grassroots level to fulfill His purposes. Jesus values people. He has called us to look at people and see the Father working in those whom the Lord has placed in our lives.

Jesus only did what He saw His Father doing and He calls us to do the same. When we find that which the Father is doing, we can then respond without pressure and we can get in the river of His anointing and flow with Him. We desire to be motivated by the kingdom, which is righteousness, peace and joy in the Holy Spirit.

In order to contribute the most to God's overall purpose for us, we are committed to continuing the wholehearted pursuit of the specific vision and calling that God has given us—to build the church with an "underground" focus in the nations of the world.

The need for new wineskins once again

During the past few years, we have watched and listened to the next generation, Generation X, those 18-35 years of age. Many are feeling what we felt more than 20 years ago. They want a new wineskin, a new type of church that meets the needs of their generation. We believe wholeheartedly that it is again time for a new model of church to be built mostly by the next generation. Many of those from my generation are being called by God to be the spiritual fathers and mothers who encourage and support this next generation as they experience church in a way that is different from what we have experienced.

Generation Xer's are looking for a church experience that focuses on (1) relationships (2) authenticity (3) the freedom to be creative, and (4) intergenerational connection. They want spiritual fathers and mothers. Thousands of their generation are convinced that they can experience Christ best in the new wineskin of a "house church" that is a complete little church in itself.

Up to this time, in North America, we have seen mostly two other kinds of churches—what we call the community or mega-churches. The community church is a church of generally 50-1,000 meeting in a traditional setting of a church building on Sunday mornings. It may or may not have cell groups meeting in smaller groups during the week. The mega-church is larger, with over 1,000, and it also meets in church buildings and may or may not have cell groups as a part of it.

The new house churches are quite different from community and mega-churches. There is no need for a large church building, because each house church is a fully functioning church itself. They can meet in a variety of places including homes, places of business, school classrooms, skate parks, shopping malls, anywhere that people meet. Each house church is led not by a cell leader, but by a spiritual father or mother who functions as the elder or pastor for the little church. Each house church is committed to network together with other house churches in their city or region to keep them from pride, exclusiveness, and heresy.

House churches as true churches

Generation Xer's say they believe these new house churches in their area will meet together once every month or so for corporate worship and teaching. But this monthly celebration is not the church. The house churches are true churches, not just Bible studies or cell groups. They have elders, they collect tithes and offerings, and the leadership is responsible before the Lord for the souls of the people in the house church (Hebrews 13:17). Additionally, these young leaders are intent on the rapid reproduction of these house churches.

These new churches are like the stores in a shopping mall. Most of the little specialized stores in a shopping mall would go out of business within a year if they were left on their own and not linked to the other stores in their mall. But together, they prosper. House churches that learn to network together in a practical way in their city will experience great blessing from the Lord. Those who do not will have a tendency to become ingrown, stagnant, stop evangelizing, and become critical of the rest of the church.

Right alongside community churches and mega-churches, the Lord will raise up house churches networking together as vessels for His harvest. These house churches will have small cells for training new leaders and to give every believer the opportunity to minister. Only instead of constructing a church building, when the house or place where they are meeting in is outgrown, a new house church is planted. Dr. Peter Wagner has said so often, "The single most effective method of evangelism is to plant new churches."

House church networks—a wave of the future

Thirty years ago, home schooling was almost unheard of in America. But today, it is commonplace. All across America, some children are educated at home, some educated in a public school, while others learn in a Christian school. These three types of educational training exist together in nearly every community in America. There is no competition. All three options are legitimate. Ten years from now, we believe thousands of house churches will have emerged all across America in our cities and regions. They will network with one another, but they will also serve together with the hundreds of community churches of many flavors and varieties. Both house churches networking together and those that meet in church buildings every Sunday will serve alongside the mega-churches of our communities. God will bless all three—the house church, the community church, and the mega-church! He is raising up His church in every region. Some will worship Him as a part of a mega-church, others as a part of a smaller church in their community, while others will be involved in house churches networking together.

Looking unto Jesus, the Lord of the harvest

Like our early beginnings, we are again sensing that the harvest is upon us. The Lord, like a great magnet, is drawing people into His kingdom. Since new wineskins eventually get old, many who have been believers for years are becoming dissatisfied with life as it is in their present church structures. God's people are again thirsting for new wine and wineskins. The Lord is renewing, refreshing and reviving thousands of His people all over the world. He is requiring us to provide new wineskins for the new wine, as He brings in His harvest.

We believe as we continue to commune with the Lord and obey His voice, build together as a family of churches, and reach the lost in our generation, there is going to be a need for thousands of new houses (new community churches, new mega-churches and new house church networks) and new rooms (new cell groups). Every generation is different and has different needs and preferences. We are committed to empowering, releasing, and supporting the next generation among us as they fulfill their call in God. As Elisha received a double portion of Elijah's anointing, we want to see our spiritual children far exceeding us in their depth of spiritual experience and church leadership. Believers will be called to various areas of leadership: some to cell group leadership, others to local church leadership, others to fivefold ministry, and others will serve in apostolic leadership.

Now is the time to prepare leaders for the coming harvest. We cannot force new Christians into our old wineskins—we must prepare new wineskins for the new wine. Forming new vessels will facilitate the Lord's commission to make disciples. Many new types of vessels, including new house churches networking together in our communities, must be formed. Let's get about our Father's business.